PRAISE FOR *40 WAYS TO DI*
THE HISTORY CURRICU

This book is a must-read for any teacher of history, offering detailed, practical and insightful advice on diversifying the curriculum. These are not 'top tips' or tokenistic gestures of representation, but deeply thoughtful suggestions linking to second-order concepts which will help students understand how, as the author makes clear in her introduction, identity and representation matter in shaping our sense of self, our communities and the ways in which our conception of the world is constructed. In doing so, Elena Stevens doesn't simply introduce us to people and situations we may have been ignorant of, but she offers a way of making us all better historians along the way. And, it would not be too much to claim, better human beings too.

Dr Debra Kidd, author and teacher

Designing a history curriculum is a fraught activity, with an unmanageably wide canvas to draw from and every decision saying something about the relevance, or significance, or impact of a particular event, person or period. An additional limitation is provided by what is already known to the teachers – not only can you not teach what you don't know, but it's also almost impossible to go looking efficiently if you don't know where to start. To this end, Elena Stevens' book is invaluable. If you are looking to move your curriculum beyond 'our island story', then *40 Ways to Diversify the History Curriculum* offers you a treasure trove of starting points: historical nuggets that have been looked over by a practised teacher's eye and are accompanied by suggestions for enabling the stories to capture students' learning and to swiftly develop their historical skills of enquiry and reflection. This is a fascinating resource that will send you off reading more about the questions that capture your imagination – there's something new here for everyone to find.

James Handscombe, Executive Principal,
Harris Westminster Sixth Form and Harris Clapham Sixth Form

This is a timely and inspiring book which provides history teachers and educators with excellent theoretical and practical advice on how to diversify their curricula. Not only does Elena Stevens provide a clear rationale on why we should diversify many different areas of the 'traditional curriculum' but, crucially, she also offers many practical ideas, strategies and even enquiries to inspire teachers to help create a curriculum fit for the twenty-first century.

40 Ways to Diversify the History Curriculum is a real, practical guidebook that should be a core text in all history departments.

Richard McFahn, Lecturer in History Education, University of Sussex, consultant and founder of www.historyresourcecupboard.com and www.practicalhistories.com

ELENA STEVENS

40 WAYS TO DIVERSIFY THE HISTORY CURRICULUM

A PRACTICAL HANDBOOK

Crown House Publishing Limited
www.crownhouse.co.uk

First published by
Crown House Publishing Limited
Crown Buildings, Bancyfelin, Carmarthen, Wales, SA33 5ND, UK
www.crownhouse.co.uk

and

Crown House Publishing Company LLC
PO Box 2223, Williston, VT 05495, USA
www.crownhousepublishing.com

British Library Cataloguing-in-Publication Data

A catalogue entry for this book is available from the British Library.

Print ISBN 978-178583630-5
Mobi ISBN 978-178583635-0
ePub ISBN 978-178583636-7
ePDF ISBN 978-178583637-4

LCCN 2022930824

Printed and bound in the UK by
TJ Books, Padstow, Cornwall

CONTENTS

ACKNOWLEDGEMENTS

I would like to thank my husband Jarek – first, for telling me the story of Jan Flisiak and second, for his constant support and patience whilst I was working on this book.

Thanks are also due to the many teachers and writers who have championed the cause for a more diverse and inclusive curriculum, and whose work has inspired me to rethink my own teaching. I hope this book adds something useful to the diversifying project!

INTRODUCTION

In 1989, historian Arthur Marwick outlined the essential role that history plays in the construction of identity. Marwick argued that neither individuals, communities nor societies could exist without knowledge of the past: 'Without memory, individuals find great difficulty in relating to others, in finding their bearings, in taking intelligent decisions – they have often lost their sense of identity. A society without history would be in a similar condition … . A society without memory … would be a society adrift.'[1]

History as a school subject has great potential for helping to develop pupils' identities. It provides opportunities to engage with ideas, values and practices in such a manner that – many education writers suggest – equips young people to navigate the challenges of adult life.[2] History offers young people the chance, as Marwick put it, to find 'their bearings', or to anchor themselves in the present whilst claiming inspiration and affirmation from the past. Helping pupils to do this seems to be one of the most important goals of history education.

However, it is important that we carefully consider the types of identities we want to help pupils to develop, and the histories that might be chosen to promote such a project. The nature of our multicultural society demands a broadening of traditional understandings of Britishness, and recent cultural and political events (including developments in the Black Lives Matter movement, prompted by the murder of George Floyd and the toppling of the Edward Colston statue) have challenged us as teachers to rethink the ways in which we transmit notions of local, national and even global identity. We realise the need to construct curricula that reflect the diversity of society around us; to plan enquiries that acknowledge a range of perspectives, yet remain accessible and engaging, and to teach lessons that are firmly historical – rather than political, ideological or civic. Faced with such challenges, however, it can be difficult to know where to begin.

This book aims to provide history teachers with ideas and strategies for diversifying the curriculum and for weaving new, unfamiliar voices into topics that are

---

1   Arthur Marwick, *The Nature of History* (New York: Macmillan, 1989), p. 14.
2   For example, Keith C. Barton and Linda S. Levstik claim that history promotes 'democratic citizenship'. See Keith C. Barton and Linda S. Levstik, *Teaching History for the Common Good* (Abingdon: Routledge, 2004), p. 35.

widely taught in secondary schools. It outlines forty case studies that represent starting points for introducing new or perhaps overlooked individuals into teaching at Key Stages 3, 4 and 5. Reflecting the diversity of pupils' own backgrounds as well as that of British society, it helps teachers to expose the presence of women, the working classes, Black, Asian, minority ethnic, disabled and LGBTQ+ communities in the past, as a means of pluralising and opening up notions of identity. It is intended as a contribution to the decolonising project that has swept through history education in the last few years, although the individuals included in the book have not been chosen because they represent a particular political or theoretical viewpoint; instead, they act as alternative lenses through which to teach popular topics and episodes of history.

Debate about the selection of content within the history curriculum has been ongoing since the introduction of the first national curriculum in England in 1988. Recently, it has come to focus on the importance of broadening frames of reference to include non-British and non-European histories, and to move beyond the traditional narratives of power, nationality and political action – a curriculum characterised by historian Peter Mandler as 'Hitler and the Henries'.[3] Much of this debate has emerged in response to the perceived failings of the national curriculum's most recent iteration. In 2010, Michael Gove's espousal of the 'island story' sought to move the history curriculum in a rather exclusionist, self-congratulatory direction. As secretary of state for education, Gove argued that the existing history curriculum denied pupils the opportunity to learn 'one of the most inspiring stories I know – the history of our United Kingdom'.[4] Though Gove's draft curriculum was hewn of some of its more jingoistic overtones, the final 2013 curriculum nevertheless prescribed a diet composed largely of British history. Reference was made to a 'significant society or issue in world history', but this seems to have been envisaged as something of an adjunct to the more coherent history of 'these islands' from 'the earliest times to the present day'.[5]

Pupils do, of course, need to develop an understanding of the societies in which they live. It is important that history lessons help young people to gain a sense of place, and to appreciate the social, political and cultural forces that shape modern

3   Peter Mandler, 'History, National Life and the New Curriculum', *Schools History Project* (23 December 2015). Available at: http://www.schoolshistoryproject.co.uk/ResourceBase/downloads/MandlerKeynote2013.pdf.
4   Michael Gove, 'All pupils will learn our island story', Conservative Party conference [speech] (5 October 2010). Available at: https://conservative-speeches.sayit.mysociety.org/speech/601441.
5   Department for Education, *History Programmes of Study: Key Stage 3* (2013), p. 1–5. Ref: DFE-00194-2013. Available at: https://assets.publishing.service.gov.uk/government/uploads/system/uploads/attachment_data/file/239075/SECONDARY_national_curriculum_-_History.pdf.

British life. However, two aspects of Gove's vision are problematic. The first is the notion that the history of our United Kingdom and world history are distinct from one another. The story of Britain is the story of movement, heterogeneity and integration; Britain has been shaped by successive invasions and migrations, and different peoples have coexisted for hundreds, if not thousands, of years. British history *is* world history. Secondly, Gove presumes that 'our island story' is one that ought to 'inspire' pupils, with its litany of heroic characters conceived as contemporary role models. In reality, the history of Britain and British people is much more complicated. It is punctuated with stories of exploitation, violence, corruption and rejection. It is also strewn with complex individuals, whose lives cannot be taken to exemplify a certain theme, idea or experience. People in the past did not exist simply to stand for one thing or another, and it does a disservice to these people's lives (and to the discipline of history) if we reduce them to archetypes or caricatures.

The best history is history that illuminates the complexity of the past. History is an exciting, dynamic discipline; new evidence and interpretation can offer up perspectives that shift our understanding, or make us think about events, people or ideas in new ways. The same is true of history teaching. If our lessons can expose pupils to new histories – or even shed new light on histories with which young people have become familiar by the time they enter our classrooms – then we have gone some way towards exposing the complexity of history. This mission was summed up well in the Swann Report of 1985, which commented on the education of children from minority ethnic backgrounds. The report concluded that education ought to represent 'something more than the reinforcement of the beliefs, values and identity which each child brings to school'.[6] History lessons can serve a vital role in challenging preconceived ideas about people in both the past and the present, equipping young people to combat deeper and more problematic misconceptions.

Of course, we do not operate within a policy vacuum; as teachers we are guided by the recommendations made by the Swann Report and other documents. For example, the Race Relations (Amendment) Act (2000) stipulated that schools must actively promote race equality and relations between people of different racial

---

6   Committee of Enquiry into the Education of Children from Ethnic Minority Backgrounds, *The Swann Report* (1985), p. 364. Available at: http://www.educationengland.org.uk/documents/swann/swann1985.html. According to the report, this mission would help to 'combat racism' and 'attack inherited myths and stereotypes'.

groups.[7] The Equality Act (2010) clarified the unlawful nature of both racial and gender discrimination, providing schools with guidance for the advancement of equal opportunities for all pupils.[8] Though the implications of such policies are evident on a school-wide level, there will be plenty of opportunities to address these priorities within the history curriculum – and, indeed, to help to advance a more nuanced understanding of race, equality and discrimination as both historical and contemporary concepts.

The case studies offered in this book aim to complicate aspects of Gove's 'island story', and to enhance pupils' experiences of diversity and equality within the curriculum. I think it is important for pupils to understand *why* certain histories are chosen or prioritised, too. As Christine Counsell explains in the chapter 'History' (part of a 2021 edited volume entitled *What Should Schools Teach? Discipline, Subjects and the Pursuit of Truth*), the selection and transmission of all stories is an 'interpretive process'; it is essential that pupils develop some understanding of the discipline of history, and the processes that contribute to its formation.[9] As such, the case studies included in this book often provide opportunities for building activities that make visible the historiography surrounding the individual or topic. Discussion might be initiated, for example, on the ways in which members of society, public commentators and historians have viewed people like Emma Hamilton or the Chevalier d'Eon in the past, to help pupils recognise some of the ways in which historical interpretation might change depending on the social, cultural, political or ideological context. In this way, the case studies aim to strike a balance between content knowledge and disciplinary awareness, recognising that knowledge is – to some extent – 'constructed'.[10]

Counsell also underlines the power of well-chosen disciplinary frameworks for the delivery of contested histories. Referencing the history website *Another History is Possible*,[11] she recounts one history teacher's decision to switch from the causation-focused question 'Why was slavery abolished in 1833?' to the change/

---

7   See https://www.legislation.gov.uk/ukpga/2000/34/enacted.
8   See https://www.legislation.gov.uk/ukpga/2010/15/contents.
9   Christine Counsell, 'History'. In Alka Sehgal Cuthbert and Alex Standish (eds) *What Should Schools Teach? Disciplines, Subjects and the Pursuit of Truth*, 2nd edn (London: UCL Press, 2021), pp. 154–173 at p. 156.
10 Nick Dennis, 'The Stories We Tell Ourselves: History Teaching, Powerful Knowledge and the Importance of Context'. In Arthur Chapman (ed.), *Knowing History in Schools: Powerful Knowledge and the Powers of Knowledge* (London: UCL Press, 2021), pp. 216–233 at pp. 218–219. Citing the work of Michael Young, Nick Dennis argues for the benefits of history education that charts a route between the transmission of knowledge (referred to as 'Future 1') and the rejection of the status of all knowledge ('Future 2'). Young's 'Future 3' rejects the idea of knowledge 'as a given', recognising that 'there is an element of construction regarding knowledge, which is fallible and open to change'.
11 See https://anotherhistoryispossible.com/.

continuity question 'Was there more continuity than change in British–Jamaican relations between 1760 and 1870?'. Counsell argues that the new question helped to complicate the notion of an uninterrupted forward trajectory in the abolition movement, as well as making space for formerly neglected stories of Black agency.[12] The framing of appropriate questions is important, then – and in this book, many of the enquiry questions either reference the idea of interpretation, or draw upon the second-order concept of significance as a means of making explicit the problematic claims that have been made about certain individuals in the past, as well as the rationale behind exploring their stories from alternative points of view.

The events of 2020 and 2021 have underlined the importance of challenging received histories of empire, slavery, abolition and race, in particular. The murder of George Floyd by a police officer in Minneapolis, Minnesota in May 2020 sparked global outrage and inspired a wave of activism; many protestors marched and campaigned in the name of Black Lives Matter, a movement which – since 2013 – has worked to bring about justice and an end to racism. In the UK, a number of protestors tore down or defaced several statues dedicated to individuals who had links to the slave trade – most notably, a statue depicting the Bristol merchant and slave trader Edward Colston. Some commentators have likened the impact of George Floyd with that of Rosa Parks and Emmett Till, suggesting that these individuals all provided the fuel for a global race movement. Of course, in the case of George Floyd it was the collective uproar on social media (particularly Twitter) that really helped to funnel public anger at the specific injustice into broader calls for political, institutional and cultural change.[13] In the wake of these activities, schools were urged to rethink the manner in which certain histories were delivered. The notion of decolonising the curriculum (already established as an area of focus within university and academic circles) was popularised, and Twitter was awash with initiatives and inspiration for rethinking the manner in which Black history is delivered within British schools.[14]

For me, the most important message to come out of the recent decolonising initiatives has been the importance of allowing lessons, activities and enquiries to be

12 Counsell, 'History', p. 158.
13 Mary Blankenship and Richard V. Reeves, 'From the George Floyd Moment to a Black Lives Matter Movement, in Tweets', *Brookings* (10 July 2020). Available at: https://www.brookings.edu/blog/up-front/2020/07/10/from-the-george-floyd-moment-to-a-black-lives-matter-movement-in-tweets/.
14 For an overview of some of these demands for change, see Matt Bromley, 'Black Lives Matter: How Schools Must Respond', *SecEd* (25 November 2020). Available at: https://www.sec-ed.co.uk/best-practice/black-lives-matter-how-schools-must-respond-curriculum-racism-george-floyd-teaching-colston/.

led by the stories or histories that are being introduced. It is not simply a case of inserting a Black abolitionist campaigner into a scheme of work on the abolition movement, or a female scientist into an enquiry on the development of modern medicine; truly diverse, decolonised history is not built on tokenistic reference to marginalised individuals simply for the sake of it. Doing so would only underline the impression that certain identities are peripheral to the story of British life and society. Instead, the decolonising project has taught us that these histories – as well as our pupils – are best served by incorporating the experiences of over-looked individuals into the main narrative, and even allowing these individuals' stories to alter this narrative, if necessary. Quoting the work of Michael Rothberg, Nick Dennis refers to this as 'multidirectional' history. Rather than viewing, for example, Black history as 'separate, superficial and distracting from the *real* history that needs to be taught', the approach involves constant reappraisal, renegotiation and cross-referencing of the past, facilitating greater creativity and complexity when it comes to planning and re-planning schemes of work.[15]

The same is true of women's history and histories of gender and sexuality; it is important to avoid creating the impression that the experiences of women, for example, were (or are) necessarily distinct simply because of their gender, or that it is only relevant to explore the lives of women through certain historical prisms (like social and domestic history, for example). This problem was recognised by Mary Kay Thompson Tetreault in 1985, when an investigation into depictions of women in American high-school history textbooks highlighted a tendency to explore the contributions of 'notable women' or to focus simply on the ways in which well-known or exceptional women have overcome oppression – approaches that Tetreault referred to as 'compensatory' or 'bi-focal' history. Tetreault found very little evidence of 'multi-focal, relational' history – a much more desirable approach, according to which women's and men's experiences are explored as part of a 'holistic view of human experience'.[16] Adopting the former approach not only risks the dissemination of skewed, unrealistic models of femininity, but it also gives the impression that there exist separate spheres of male and female history. It suggests that whilst men have existed (and continue to exist) in the public spheres of politics, power and commerce, women are generally confined to the

---

15 Nick Dennis, 'Beyond Tokenism: Teaching a Diverse History in the Post-14 Curriculum', *Teaching History* 165 (2016): 37–41 at 37–38.
16 Mary Kay Thompson Tetreault, 'Integrating Women's History: The Case of United States History High School Textbooks', *The History Teacher* 19(2) (1986): 211–62 at 215–217.

private worlds of marriage and domesticity – and are only worthy of serious study when they manage to transgress these domains.

In a 2016 edition of *Teaching History*, Bridget Lockyer and Abigail Tazzymant examine lingering misconceptions concerning the place of women in history. They conclude that, in spite of curriculum changes and wider initiatives, the 'dominant narrative' remains that 'men (or at least a certain type of man) and men's experiences are presented as the norm, women as the *other* and ultimately a distraction.'[17] Lockyer and Tazzymant offer some useful suggestions for ways in which this might be challenged, including the use of women's history to explore 'larger themes', and the explicit investigation of stereotypes.[18]

Some inspiring work has, therefore, already been done by writers and teachers wishing to diversify or complicate the delivery of content relating to marginalised histories. Where this book differs is that it aims to introduce characters and stories that might enrich existing topics – particularly those commonly taught at Key Stages 3, 4 or 5. Whilst there are opportunities for building longer enquiries around the case studies outlined (and these opportunities are indicated throughout the book), it is recognised that the process of curriculum development is a time-consuming one, and making small additions and changes across the curriculum is sometimes more realistic (and, in fact, more impactful) than attempting to entirely overhaul a topic or unit. This book aims to provide ideas and activities that can be implemented in the short term, as well as pointing to resources that might be explored by teachers wishing to develop the case studies into deeper or broader enquiries – or, indeed, teachers wishing to hinge entire topics off of the individuals explored within these pages. For each of the suggested enquiry questions listed (two for each case study), the second-order concept through which the enquiry might be most easily taught is also given; this might be significance, causation, consequence, change and continuity, similarity and difference, evidential understanding or interpretations. A summary of some suggested activities is given for at least one of the two enquiry questions listed per case study, and the footnotes, bibliography and final chapter (Conclusion: Planning for a Diverse Curriculum) point towards resources that might be used by teachers wishing to plan their own enquiries around the case studies.

---

17 Bridget Lockyer and Abigail Tazzymant, "'Victims of History': Challenging Students' Perceptions of Women in History', *Teaching History* 165 (2016): 8–15 at 14.
18 Lockyer et al., "Victims of History", p. 14.

The book is organised according to six different themes, with a number of case studies contained within each. Increasingly, it seems that teachers and departments are structuring their Key Stage 3 curricula by theme – perhaps partly in response to the introduction of the thematic unit at GCSE, which typically requires pupils to assess the changing nature of health, power, migration, warfare or crime and punishment over time. History at Key Stage 3 often explores the changing nature of, for example, power; pupils might examine the power of monarchy in Year 7, before going on to examine the shifting nature of political power in industrial and modern Britain in Years 8 or 9. Similarly, the theme of conflict is either explicitly or implicitly present in pupils' exploration of the English and/or American Civil Wars, the French Revolution and World Wars One and Two. Migration is an increasingly popular choice for the GCSE thematic unit, and this book suggests ways in which this theme might be explored at Key Stage 3 – or, indeed, enriched at Key Stage 4 with new and insightful case studies. Particular emphasis is also lent to society and culture – themes that can sometimes be sidelined, but which present fruitful opportunities for broadening the diet of history that pupils receive at secondary school.

In line with the diversifying ethos of the book, the case studies presented here do not represent *notable* individuals. Although some of their experiences may appear extraordinary from our modern vantage points, many of the individuals would probably have considered themselves to have led rather ordinary lives. Their names would not generally appear within lists or encyclopedias of significant figures from history and, more often than not, I learnt of their stories by accident, perhaps as part of a different piece of research. This, really, is the whole point: if we want to lay claim to a truly diverse curriculum, we need to make room for stories that move beyond the traditional focus on heroes, conquerors and pioneers, exploring instead the real, lived experiences of a whole range of individuals. Fundamentally, we also need to emphasise the value of these kinds of stories, encouraging pupils to conceive of history in the broadest possible terms. By adopting such an approach, pupils will begin to recognise themselves in the people of the past – and this will prove invaluable in the process of identity construction in the present.

Dido Elizabeth Belle, see page 17

Chapter 1
EMPIRE AND SLAVERY

INTRODUCTION

Perhaps more than any other topic or area of teaching, the British Empire has been the subject of significant revision and reappraisal in recent years. This reflects the profession's engagement with contemporary events and academic developments, as teachers come to recognise that existing frameworks for delivering lessons on empire and slavery are neither appropriate nor sufficient. There is an increasing demand for activities and case studies that serve, variously, to emphasise the role and agency of the enslaved in bringing about abolition (and not only through violent means), to underline the extent to which British/colonial wealth was facilitated by exploitation and enslavement, and to acknowledge the far-reaching, varied legacies of imperialism amongst formerly colonised nations and communities.

In this context, the stated aim of the *History Programmes of Study: Key Stage 3* document – according to which, pupils are expected to develop an understanding of 'the expansion and dissolution of empires'[1] – seems problematic, placing too much emphasis on the experiences and achievements of the colonisers at the expense of the colonised. Indeed, the notion that 'Indian independence and end of Empire' might feature within a study of 'challenges for Britain, Europe and the wider world'[2] is even more troubling, lending the impression that it was the British who suffered the most damaging consequences of decolonisation. However, one aspect of the document does remain useful in light of new and developing approaches to the teaching of empire: namely, the stated aim that pupils 'gain and deploy a historically grounded understanding of abstract terms such as *empire*.'[3] When planning lessons or schemes of work that focus, perhaps, on the growth of the British Empire and the emergence of slavery as a form of international commerce, it is important to build in opportunities for pupils to really engage with the concept of empire. Pupils need to understand the political, cultural, economic and intellectual processes that have underpinned empire; they also need to grapple with the historical peculiarities of contrasting empires, and to appreciate the diverse ways in which different kinds of people experienced the imperial project.

The case studies featured in this section are intended to highlight new or neglected aspects of empire and slavery. Each reflects the historical reality in the

---

1 Department for Education, *History Programmes of Study: Key Stage 3*, p. 1.
2 Department for Education, *History Programmes of Study: Key Stage 3*, p. 4.
3 Department for Education, *History Programmes of Study: Key Stage 3*, p. 1.

sense that the exploitation of colonial subjects and enslaved men and women is highlighted. However, the case studies aim to underline the agency and individuality of those featured. They linger in particular upon acts of resistance or moments of challenge – and they aim, fundamentally, to indicate ways in which we might complicate received ideas about the individuals who were caught up in the realisation of the imperial project.

EXHIBITING THE EMPIRE: SARAH BAARTMAN/THE HOTTENTOT VENUS

Suggested enquiry: What can we learn from colonial exhibitions about attitudes towards the British Empire in the eighteenth and nineteenth centuries? (Similarity and difference/Consequence)

Alternative enquiry: What is the best way for us to remember Sarah Baartman? (Significance)

The story of Sarah Baartman – who became known derogatively as the Hottentot Venus – offers an important cultural lens through which to explore conceptions of empire at a time when the British Empire was at its height. It also allows us to convey the highly gendered ways in which bodies (especially Black bodies) were understood in the eighteenth and nineteenth centuries, as ideas of beauty, utility and ownership were shaped by ongoing debates about the moral rectitude of slavery.

Sarah (or Saartje) Baartman was born in 1789 in what is now the Eastern Cape of South Africa, at a time when the Cape Colony was under Dutch rule. Sarah was forced to travel to Britain when a Scottish visitor to the Cape – Alexander Dunlop – indicated that Baartman could be exhibited on the London stage as a curiosity. Curiosities (or, to borrow the more commonly used term, *freaks*) were a staple of popular entertainment at this time, with variety theatre bills regularly featuring *giants*, *dwarves* and *bearded women*. However, Baartman's particular appeal lay simply in her foreignness, and in her apparent exemplification of her race – particularly in her curvaceous physical appearance. In this respect, Baartman's appearance on the London stage can be situated within the context of a growing appetite for colonial exhibitions, which saw groups of *natives* imported from Britain's colonies to be displayed as living exhibits.

WHAT CAN WE LEARN FROM COLONIAL EXHIBITIONS ABOUT ATTITUDES TOWARDS THE EMPIRE IN THE EIGHTEENTH AND NINETEENTH CENTURIES? (SIMILARITY AND DIFFERENCE/CONSEQUENCE)

This enquiry might therefore begin with an examination of sources describing Baartman and her performances.[4] Pictorial representations are shocking to modern audiences, although written reviews offer even more useful opportunity to dissect the language of racial superiority/inferiority. Subsequently, pupils might explore the court case surrounding Baartman's exhibition, which – centering on the claim that Baartman was being exposed in a near-naked state without her consent – called upon precedents set by the Slave Trade Act (1807) to affirm Baartman's exploitation. The fact that the court case was quashed demonstrates the limited progress made by anti-slavery laws and campaigners in altering public attitudes.

Tragically, Sarah Baartman died at the age of 26, without ever having been permitted to record her own feelings about her experiences. However, there are a limited number of other performers whose thoughts and feelings were recorded for posterity. The voices of these individuals can be extremely powerful, serving to disrupt notions of colonial passivity and reminding pupils that there were instances of resistance or defiance amongst the supposedly disempowered. For example, the writings of T. N. Mukharji undermined the neat categorisation of *natives* as colonial exhibits, challenging the notion – influentially expressed by theorist Edward Said in *Orientalism* – that 'the Other' could not 'speak'. Said described 'Orientalism' as a 'western style for dominating, restructuring, and having authority over the Orient': essentially, the Orient was prevented from defining itself.[5] Mukharji was an upper-class Bengali deputed to London to assist in the

---

4   See Sadiah Qureshi, 'Displaying Sarah Baartman, the "Hottentot Venus"', *History of Science* 42(2) (2004): 233–257. This article outlines contemporary attitudes towards Baartman, pointing towards a range of useful contemporary sources. A BBC article offers further information: see Justin Parkinson, 'The Significance of Sarah Baartman', *BBC News* (7 January 2016). Available at: https://www.bbc.co.uk/news/magazine-35240987.
5   Edward Said, *Orientalism: Western Conceptions of the Orient* (London: Penguin, 2016 [1978]), p. 3.

planning of a *native* village set up at the Colonial and Indian Exhibition of 1886.[6] Upon his return to India, he documented his experiences in the book *A Visit to Europe* (1889).[7] Pupils might be asked to consider how organisers hoped that visitors might read the exhibitions of native people, by examining extracts from the 1886 Colonial and Indian Exhibition's catalogue.[8] Provide pupils with a grid to record their ideas: the first column can contain pupils' inferences from the catalogue about how visitors were supposed to interpret the native villages (pupils might need to be guided in coming up with these); the second column might give pupils the chance to note down ways in which Mukharji challenged these ideas. They might note, for example, Mukharji's observations of British society, and his intelligent reflections on British politics. When questioned about the apparently polygamous nature of Indian society, Mukharji good-humouredly informed a British waitress that he had killed his fortieth wife 'because one morning she could not cook my porridge well'; pupils might be guided to recognise this as evidence of Mukharji's frustration with ill-informed British stereotypes.[9] Having completed this task, pupils ought to be more attuned to the problematic and, at times, deeply disturbing nature of British attempts to define and package natives for an undiscerning public.

Placing formerly silenced individuals at the centre of an enquiry into the British Empire is essential if pupils are to grasp the full ramifications of the imperial project for the colonised. The experiences of Sarah Baartman and T. N. Mukharji help to underline the mutually reinforcing relationships that existed between scientific and political ideas of empire and race and the public presentation of natives on the stage. As politicians, writers and (pseudo)scientists justified colonial subjugation on the grounds of physical, social and cultural hierarchy, entertainment impresarios helped to ensure that ordinary Britons understood natives as immutably inferior – and, therefore, deserving of their enslavement. Individuals like Mukharji serve to challenge these hierarchies in some ways – although an enquiry focused on the imperial project ought, fundamentally, to emphasise these individuals' powerlessness in challenging such a rigid and self-serving system as the British Empire.

6   For more about colonial exhibits, see Peter Hoffenberg, *An Empire on Display: English, Indian, and Australian Exhibitions from the Crystal Palace to the Great War* (Berkeley, CA: University of California Press, 2001). Hoffenberg describes the colonial villages, noting that they transformed distant lands into 'a series of images expressed in an aesthetic grammar for observation and consumption', allowing British visitors to feel superiority over distant lands and their inhabitants (p. 71).
7   T. N. Mukharji, *A Visit to Europe* (Calcutta: W. Newman & Co., 1889).
8   Thomas Wardle, *Colonial and Indian Exhibition, 1886* (London: William Clowes & Sons, 1886).
9   Mukharji, *A Visit*, p. 100.

KEY POINTS

- Born in South Africa in 1789, Sarah Baartman was made to perform on the London stage as a curiosity act.

- Colonial exhibitions were popular in the late eighteenth and nineteenth centuries, with natives displayed as living exhibits.

- Some of those categorised as natives (like T. N. Mukharji) had greater agency than Baartman.

- Baartman's experiences in Britain exemplified British attitudes towards the colonised.

'NEITHER HANDSOME NOR GENTEEL': DIDO ELIZABETH BELLE

- **Suggested enquiry:** How accurately did David Martin's portrait represent the lives of enslaved and formerly enslaved people in Britain? (Interpretations)

- **Alternative enquiry:** How did attitudes towards slavery change during the eighteenth and nineteenth centuries? (Change and continuity)

In the 1770s, the Earl and Countess of Mansfield commissioned a very unusual painting. The painting – a portrait – depicted their great-niece, Lady Elizabeth Murray, delicately clasping an open book as she perched on a bench (so far, so conventional). To the side of Elizabeth, however – and far less conventionally – was depicted a young Black woman, also dressed in the elegant finery of eighteenth-century polite society. Elizabeth's right hand extends towards her companion, the warm gesture indicating companionship and perhaps even a kind of dependence. The two women appear as near-equals; although Elizabeth is positioned slightly closer to the painting's foreground, the viewer's eye is neither drawn more to one woman or the other.

The woman depicted alongside Elizabeth Murray was Dido Elizabeth Belle, the daughter of an enslaved woman and a British naval officer. Born into slavery herself, Belle was taken to England by her father and entrusted to the care of her great-uncle and his wife (the Mansfields). She grew up at the earl and countess' country house in Hampstead, where Elizabeth Murray (whose own mother had died) was also being raised. Though ostensibly employed as Elizabeth Murray's personal attendant, evidence suggests that Belle's relationship with her cousin was founded more in friendship than in duty. Additionally, the Earl of Mansfield served for over thirty years as lord chief justice (the most powerful judge in England), and he presided over several cases relating to the slave trade. Belle even dictated some of his letters for him, so may have been privy to documents describing the experiences of enslaved individuals. In one significant case of 1772, Mansfield ruled that slaveholders were not able to send slaves in England out of the country to be sold in places like Jamaica.[10] It is possible that this ruling (a key moment in the early abolition movement) was influenced by Mansfield's own relationship with Belle.

HOW ACCURATELY DID DAVID MARTIN'S PORTRAIT REPRESENT THE LIVES OF ENSLAVED AND FORMERLY ENSLAVED PEOPLE IN BRITAIN? (INTERPRETATIONS)

Portraits such as that of Belle and her cousin are a useful way of engaging pupils in the task of imaginative reconstruction. Of course, these images offer only a limited number of clues – some of which can be either intentionally or unintentionally misleading. However, examining these clues alongside other fragments of evidence allows us to piece together an understanding of what it might have been like to live in a particular time or place in history.

Pupils might therefore begin their study of Dido Elizabeth Belle by examining the portrait in question. Painted in 1778, the portrait has been variously attributed to Johan Zoffany and Joshua Reynolds, although historians now believe that the Mansfields commissioned Scottish artist David Martin to complete it. Pupils may be asked to consider why the portrait was so unusual for its time. It is important they are guided to recognise that it was not so much Belle's inclusion in the portrait that was unusual, as Black men, women and children often featured as liveried servants in late-eighteenth century family portraits. It was rather more unusual that Belle was depicted as a near-equal of her white companion, wearing clothing indicative of her own status and wealth. Features like Belle's turban and the bouquet of exotic fruits and flowers can be discussed, as can the fact that Belle is

---

10 Gene Adams, 'Dido Elizabeth Belle: A Black Girl at Kenwood', *Camden History Review* 12 (1984): 2. Available at: http://www.mirandakaufmann.com/uploads/1/2/2/5/12258270/dido-elizabeth-belle_-a-black-girl-at-kenwood.pdf.

pointing to her own face.[11] Some commentators have suggested that the artist wanted to draw attention to the subject's skin colour, whilst others have concluded that Belle was depicted pointing to her expression – a smile – as an indication of her happy acceptance into British society.

Subsequently, pupils can examine other clues relating to Belle's experiences, including information about her mother, Maria Belle, and about Belle's life at the Mansfields' country house, where – despite the gentle disapprobation of friends (she was 'neither handsome nor genteel', said American politician Thomas Hutchinson[12]) – she received an education, an annual allowance and many of the privileges of a free gentlewoman. It is useful to ask pupils to come up with four or five adjectives to best characterise Belle's life in Britain, as a way of cementing pupils' understanding. The final stage of the enquiry might see pupils develop a broader awareness of the lives of enslaved and formerly enslaved individuals in Britain towards the end of the eighteenth century. Provide a grid to help pupils organise their ideas. Themes for pupils to investigate might include working life, family life, acceptance and integration, and challenges. Having completed this activity, pupils are likely to realise that David Martin's painting is misleadingly optimistic; racist stereotypes remained highly pervasive and influential, shaping the lives of the free and the unfree alike.

Belle's story can therefore be used to add nuance and complexity to the study of slavery and its wide-ranging consequences for the enslaved. It allows us to complicate the story of abolition, too – a story so often recalled as one of inexorable progress, with the great and good of British society supposedly championing the freedoms of the oppressed. Indeed, the very atypicality of David Martin's portrait shows that most British elites were extremely reluctant to advocate for the rights of the enslaved or formerly enslaved, with the social and material benefits of the system far outweighing the admission of any moral qualms.

KEY POINTS

- The daughter of an enslaved woman and a naval officer, Dido Elizabeth Belle was brought up in Britain by the Earl and Countess of Mansfield.

---

11 See Kenna Libes, '1778 – David Martin, Portrait of Dido Elizabeth Belle Lindsay and Lady Elizabeth Murray', *Fashion History Timeline* (3 August 2020). Available at: https://fashionhistory.fitnyc. edu/1778-martin-dido-elizabeth/. Libes offers context for Martin's portrait, giving particularly useful insight into late-eighteenth century fashion.
12 Adams, 'Dido Elizabeth Belle: A Black Girl at Kenwood', p. 1.

- Belle was painted alongside her companion Lady Elizabeth Murray in a portrait by David Martin.

- Belle's story allows us to explore attitudes towards slavery and abolition in the late eighteenth century.

- Portraits help pupils to imaginatively reconstruct the past.

THE PORTCHESTER PRISONERS

> ● **Suggested enquiry:** What can we learn from General Marinier about resistance to colonial rule? (Change and continuity/Significance)
>
> ● **Alternative enquiry:** Why were enslaved men and women from the Caribbean imprisoned in Portsmouth in 1796? (Causation)

In the winter of 1796, around 2,000 men, women and children from the Caribbean island of St Lucia arrived at Portchester Castle (in Portsmouth Harbour, located in south-east England). They had been part of a garrison on St Lucia, defending the island on behalf of the French Revolutionary Army which had declared an end to slavery in the early 1790s. Britain (still a slave-owning nation at this point) claimed the garrison on St Lucia, and the captives became prisoners of war. The Atlantic crossing was long and uncomfortable; reports suggested that both crewmen and captives endured terrible sickness, and at least 268 prisoners died on the voyage. When the prisoners arrived at Portchester, they were in no condition to withstand the cold English winter. Some of the prisoners suffered from frostbite; a few lost their toes. Any warm clothes the prisoners did have were liable to be stolen – most likely by European men also imprisoned at Portchester, who considered themselves 'as a superior race of beings to the unfortunate Blacks.'[13] Eventually, the men, women and children were exchanged for captured British soldiers and were sent to France. Some of the men joined the 7th Royal African Regiment, fighting on France's behalf in Italy and Russia. It is possible, too, that some of those imprisoned at Portchester were recruited into the British Army or Navy, as the British armed forces actively recruited prisoners of war as soldiers and sailors at this time.

This episode in Portchester Castle's long history can be explored through a causation enquiry in which pupils examine evidence as they try to ascertain how and why the imprisoned men, women and children ended up in Portsmouth in the late eighteenth century. The enquiry is a useful way of highlighting the extent to which

---

13 English Heritage, 'Black Prisoners of War at Portchester Castle' (n.d.). Available at: https://www.english-heritage.org.uk/visit/places/portchester-castle/history-and-stories/black-prisoners-at-portchester/.

the slave trade – and the movements to bring about its demise – resulted in ordinary men, women and children being dislocated and displaced across the globe.

WHAT CAN WE LEARN FROM GENERAL MARINIER ABOUT RESISTANCE TO COLONIAL RULE? (CHANGE AND CONTINUITY/SIGNIFICANCE)

Alternatively, an enquiry might be framed around General Marinier – a soldier of mixed ethnic background who had commanded French forces on St Lucia and who found himself imprisoned at Portchester in 1796. The enquiry might begin with pupils piecing together events in St Lucia, Britain and France. Pupils need to understand both the chronology and the geography, so asking pupils to plot the captives' activities onto a blank world map is a useful task. Next, pupils gather evidence about the experiences of Marinier and the Portchester prisoners. Provide pupils with a grid to help them record different aspects of the prisoners' experiences. The categories could be: *Actions of the resisters*, *Who were the resisters?* and *What happened to them?* Pupils learn how Marinier and his fellow prisoners' actions on St Lucia resulted in their capture, and they gain an insight into how the British treated captured Black men and women (who were conferred the status of 'prisoners of war' rather than 'slaves', although slavery was still legal in British-controlled territories). Pupils are encouraged to make inferences from sources including the recollections of the British ship's captain, the prison inspectors and the commander of the defences at Portsmouth, all of whom made reference to the Black captives at Portchester. The latter of these, General Pitt, apparently 'showed him [General Marinier] off to the local gentry, as if he were a lion':[14] Marinier was exoticised; paraded around the prison's grounds as an exemplification of his type.

Having learned about the actions and experiences of General Marinier and the Portchester prisoners, pupils might be encouraged to draw comparisons with other instances of resistance and rebellion.[15] This is an opportunity for pupils to learn

---

14 English Heritage, 'Speaking with Shadows: Transcript of Episode 2: The Caribbean Prisoners of Portchester Castle' (2019). Available at: https://www.english-heritage.org.uk/siteassets/home/visit/inspire-me/speaking-with-shadows/sws-episode-2/speaking-with-shadows-episode-2-transcript.pdf.

15 See Judith Edwards, *Fighting for Freedom: Abolitionists and Slave Resistance* (New York: Enslow Publishing, 2017). Edwards provides a concise overview of the history of resistance movements amongst enslaved individuals.

more about individuals such as Toussaint L'Ouverture and Olaudah Equiano, as well as events such as the Baptist War, Tacky's Revolt and the Haitian Revolution. Pupils ought to consider how resistance manifested itself in different ways, as they compare the actions – and efficacy – of General Marinier and other resisters and rebels.

The story of the Portchester prisoners adds flavour to our understanding of diversity in eighteenth- and nineteenth-century Britain. It also complicates widely held notions of the British as the heroes of abolition, or the bastions of moral rectitude, in an age of exploitation and enslavement. Exploring the experiences of formerly enslaved men, women and children at Portchester Castle literally brings the story of slavery, resistance and abolition home for pupils, allowing them to examine events that might otherwise feel somewhat remote (both in time and place) from their own lives. This enquiry provides a certain kind of proximity for the study of these larger narratives, underlining some of the global, national and local dimensions implicit within the histories of empire and slavery.

KEY POINTS

- In 1796, Portchester Castle housed 2,000 prisoners from St Lucia.

- The captives had defended St Lucia on behalf of the French Revolutionary Army (France having previously abolished slavery), but the island was seized by the British.

- General Marinier – one of those imprisoned at Portchester – is a case study in resistance to colonial rule.

- Enslaved men and women resisted enslavement and captivity in various ways; the story of the Portchester prisoners helps to underline this.

THE WHITE QUEEN OF OKOYONG: MARY SLESSOR

- **Suggested enquiry:** Does Mary Slessor deserve to be reinstated on the Scottish banknote? (Significance)
- **Alternative enquiry:** What can we learn from Mary Slessor about changing attitudes towards Africa? (Change and continuity)

According to an article on the Bank of England website, individuals are chosen to feature on banknotes by virtue of the 'important contribution' they have made to 'our society and culture'. In 2014, a new method for selecting these individuals saw an advisory committee select the field to be represented on newly issued notes – with 'innovation, leadership and values' representing key criteria in the selection process. Members of the public then nominated individuals within this field. This process resulted in the selection of artist J. M. W. Turner for the polymer £20 banknote, and scientist Alan Turing for the £50 note. The article also notes the Bank of England's desire for the individuals represented on banknotes to 'come from different backgrounds and fields',[16] although the range of individuals to have featured so far does not entirely reflect the diversity of modern British society and culture.

Framing an enquiry around the question 'Does [insert individual] deserve to be featured on the [insert banknote]?' is a good way of encouraging pupils to think about significance. It is interesting to share the Bank of England's selection process with pupils, encouraging them to think about how they would make the decision; what makes people from the past important enough that they deserve this kind of recognition? Depending on the topic and period studied, pupils can compare the attributes and achievements of the individual currently featured on the banknote with other candidates, using significance criteria to help them make their judgements.

16 Bank of England, 'Choosing Banknote Characters', *Bank of England* (22 June 2021). Available at: https://www.bankofengland.co.uk/banknotes/banknote-characters.

DOES MARY SLESSOR DESERVE TO BE REINSTATED ON THE SCOTTISH BANKNOTE? (SIGNIFICANCE)

In 2006, the Scottish £10 banknote featuring nineteenth-century missionary Mary Slessor was withdrawn, and a new issue featured poet Robert Burns as Slessor's replacement. Slessor had featured on the banknote since 1997 (ensconced in an *African* setting, with four Black children surrounding her – along with a map to indicate the region of modern-day Nigeria in which she worked), with an image of the missionary on the banknote's reverse. Slessor's work in spreading the messages of Christianity and safeguarding the rights of women and children in the Okoyong region of Nigeria was clearly judged significant enough to warrant Slessor's place on the banknote in 1997. So, why was she replaced by Robert Burns in the banknote's more recent issue? Does Slessor deserve to be reinstated?

Mary Slessor was born in 1848 and her childhood was a challenging one; Mary's father and brothers died of pneumonia, leaving Mary, her mother and her two sisters to struggle through life in the slums of Dundee. Slessor was raised as a devout Presbyterian and, inspired by the work of David Livingstone and other well-known missionaries, Slessor applied to the United Presbyterian Church's Foreign Missionary Board in 1876. She was sent to West Africa soon after. Slessor and her fellow missionaries arrived in Calabar, Nigeria, harbouring views typical of mid-Victorian society; Africa was held to be the dark continent, and Africans were considered unchristian – perhaps uncivilised – heathens who lacked the ability to govern themselves. Of course, these attitudes need to be unpicked; pupils ought to recognise the context in which such views came into being, including Britain's historic incursions into the region through the slave trade (which had necessitated an infantilisation of Africans as a means of morally justifying the trade's continuation), and the development of pseudoscientific ideas that depended upon the hierarchical classification of different human races. Still, Slessor's work was motivated by a genuine desire to help, as she undertook the education of men, women and children in the Calabar region and saved hundreds of babies who had been condemned to death due to the local custom of abandoning twins to either starve or be eaten by animals. She lived for fifteen years with the Okoyong people, learning the Efik language so that she could encourage local trade and settle disputes.

In Britain she became known as the White Queen of Okoyong and when she died in 1915 she received the equivalent of a state funeral in Nigeria. A statue to honour Slessor still stands in south-east Nigeria and roads, schools and hospitals in both Nigeria and Scotland bear Slessor's name.[17]

In the enquiry, pupils might gather evidence about Slessor's significance, recording their findings on a grid using these headings: *Challenges Slessor faced, Evidence of her impact at the time, Evidence of her longer-term impact.* Having done this, pupils ought to be equipped to answer the enquiry question. Pupils could write a letter to the Bank of Scotland, outlining their conclusions. Provide a word frame to help with this (and to encourage pupils to organise their ideas around clear points), i.e. *'To whom it may concern, I am writing this letter with the intention of suggesting that ... . I have reached this conclusion because ... . Therefore, I would like to see ... .'*.

Mary Slessor's story offers useful insight into Britain's changing relationship with Africa in the nineteenth century. Slave trading was coming to an end and Britain sought to establish itself on the one hand as a benevolent, Christianising force, and on the other as a contender in the European race to colonise large swathes of the continent. The enquiry raises important questions about the extent to which missionaries ought to be considered agents of British colonialism. With carefully selected sources and sensitively handled discussion, it is possible to paint a nuanced picture of both missionary work and of the Okoyong community that ultimately embraced Slessor and the values she stood for.

KEY POINTS

- Scottish missionary Mary Slessor arrived in West Africa in 1876, believing that Africans needed to be civilised through Christian education.

- Slessor saved babies who had been condemned to death, as well as encouraging local trade and settling disputes.

- Slessor's story complicates ideas about nineteenth-century missionary work.

- Framing enquiries around the individuals featured on banknotes allows pupils to explore the second-order concept of significance.

---

17 For an overview of Slessor's life and career, see Jeanette Hardage, *Mary Slessor – Everybody's Mother: The Era and Impact of a Victorian Missionary* (Eugene, OR: Wipf and Stock, 2008).

THE THREE KINGS OF BECHUANALAND

> ● **Suggested enquiry:** Why was the visit of the three kings of Bechuanaland significant? (Consequence)
>
> ● **Alternative enquiry:** Why was Cecil Rhodes so worried about the three kings of Bechuanaland? (Significance/Causation)

The year was 1895 and the three kings in question were Khama III, Bathoen I and Sebele I. All were rulers from the Bechuanaland Protectorate in modern-day Botswana. Two years previously, Cecil Rhodes – who was serving as prime minister of southern Africa's Cape Colony – had prevailed in the First Matabele War and had used his victory as an opportunity to extend control over native populations. It was clear in 1895 that the Bechuanaland Protectorate was Rhodes' next target, as the imperialist sought to bring this region under the control of the British South Africa Company – a move that would entail a loss of political autonomy for the Bechuanaland kings. Khama, Bathoen and Sebele decided that their only chance of protecting Bechuanaland against this encroachment was to appeal directly to the British government; indeed, Khama proposed to convince 'the Queen and the people of England' of the rectitude of the three kings' mission.[18] In September 1895, therefore, Khama, Batheon and Sebele embarked upon a tour of Britain, visiting Birmingham, Liverpool, Manchester, Edinburgh, Brighton and London, and meeting hundreds of local dignitaries along the way. In many respects, the tour was a triumph for the Bechuanaland kings – and a public relations disaster for Rhodes and the Cape Colony.

The tour was documented by a British press eager to emphasise the strangeness of the three Bechuanaland kings. For this reason there is a wealth of source material that might be incorporated into lessons, from photographs and newspaper

---

18 Neil Parsons, *King Khama, Emperor Joe and the Great White Queen* (Chicago, IL: University of Chicago Press, 1998), p. 51. For more about the visit of the three kings, see David Olusoga, *Black and British: A Forgotten History*, BBC [documentary] (2016). Part 4 of this series features the three kings' visit.

reports to tour programmes and records of various speeches made along the way.[19] It would be a worthwhile exercise for pupils studying the operations of the British Empire to conduct a close reading of these sources, if only to explore the ways in which the three kings successfully challenged some of the racist assumptions that underpinned the propagation of empire in the nineteenth century. However, the story of the three kings' tour offers a particularly fruitful opportunity for constructing a significance/consequence enquiry, in which pupils explore some of the ramifications of this seemingly minor event for broader developments in the Scramble for Africa.

WHY WAS THE VISIT OF THE THREE KINGS OF BECHUANALAND SIGNIFICANT? (CONSEQUENCE)

Pupils might start by examining some of the ways in which Rhodes and the Cape Colonists pictured the natives of southern Africa. Postcards and other illustrations produced during the British South Africa Company's 1891 expedition emphasise the supposedly primitive nature of the African people and were intended to justify the subjugation of Africa on both moral and pragmatic grounds. Such sources contrast well with photographs of Khama, Bathoen and Sebele that were taken during their tour of Britain, in which they appear (not unproblematically) as respectably attired Victorian gentlemen. Once pupils have studied the imperialists' vision of a conquered Africa, they can begin considering the significance of the three kings' unprecedented visit to Britain.

The significance model devised by Christine Counsell offers a useful framework for assessing the significance of the three kings' visit.[20] Pupils are tasked with identifying evidence from a range of sources that indicate the fulfilment (or otherwise) of Counsell's '5 Rs': *remarkable, remembered, resulted in change, resonant, revealing*. Provide pupils with a grid to record their information: the first column should contain Christine Counsell's significance criteria and the second should be blank to allow pupils to make their notes. Pupils might note, for example, that the

---

19 Many of these resources are available online, put together as a Black history teaching pack for schools. See Brighton & Hove Black History, 'African Kings in Brighton' (n.d.). Available at: https://black-history.org.uk/project/three-african-kings-visit-brighton-in-1895/.

20 Christine Counsell, 'Looking Through a Josephine Butler-shaped Window: Focusing Pupils' Thinking on Historical Significance', *Teaching History* 114 (2004): 30–34 at 32.

visit was very frequently *remarked upon* in contemporary newspapers and periodicals, with detailed reports of the three kings' visits to such sites as the Crystal
Palace. They might also identify the construction of a huge memorial to the three
kings in modern-day Botswana as evidence of the visit having been *remembered*;
the visit is memorialised as a landmark event in the struggle for Botswanan independence. Finally, pupils are likely to recognise that the visit helped to engender
further negotiations between the British government and Cecil Rhodes' British
South Africa Company, ultimately preventing Rhodes' annexation of the
Bechuanaland Protectorate and ensuring that the area remained under direct
British administration until Botswanan independence was granted in 1960. It
seems, then, that the significance of this short visit from three southern African
kings during the latter years of Queen Victoria's reign can barely be overstated.

This enquiry sees pupils examine the role played by three individuals in ensuring
the relative independence of the Bechuanaland Protectorate. It helps pupils to
understand the British Empire not as one sweeping entity, but as a conglomerate
of forces, ideas and personalities, some of which were becoming increasingly frac-
tured. By exploring the influence exerted by the three kings at this critical juncture,
the enquiry challenges received notions of British imperial domination at the turn
of the twentieth century.

In light of the recent debates prompted by the Black Lives Matter movement, it
might be useful for the enquiry to end with pupils exploring issues of commemoration and memorialisation in relation to Rhodes' statues in South Africa and
Britain. Debate might centre upon the role played by statues in helping to shape
certain ideas and narratives about the past – and the extent to which the history
of the British Empire is best told through statues and monuments, or through other
methods of commemoration.

KEY POINTS

- In 1895, three kings from the Bechuanaland Protectorate – Khama III,
  Bathoen I and Sebele I – arrived in Britain, seeking support against the
  expansion of Cecil Rhodes' British South Africa Company.

- The kings became celebrities and their visit was covered by the British press.

- The visit was a success: Rhodes was prevented from annexing the Bechuanaland Protectorate.

- This enquiry underlines the heterogeneity of the British Empire in the late nineteenth century.

Chapter 2
MIGRATION

Sacagawea, see page 42.

INTRODUCTION

The theme of migration has assumed a much more prominent place within Key Stage 3 and 4 curricula in recent years. The topic is now offered as a GCSE thematic study by several exam boards, and it seems to be recognised amongst history teachers that there is real scope for enriching Key Stage 3 teaching with a focus on the historic movement of peoples and ideas. Migration certainly lends itself to a thematic approach, allowing pupils to identify patterns and trends, and to draw comparisons between different types of migrations over time. However, teaching these lessons or schemes of work through case studies allows us to exemplify the real, lived experiences of those who – for various reasons – became migrants, and to underline the diversity of these migrants' experiences.

The *History Programmes of Study: Key Stage 3* document recommends that a study of migration prior to 1066 might serve to deepen pupils' 'chronological knowledge' of British history in this time period – and, perhaps, to help pupils understand the extent to which the British Isles was founded on a series of migrations.[1] The GCSE thematic studies offered by AQA, OCR and Edexcel extend the period under consideration considerably, requiring pupils to study migration from as early as c790 to the present day. Groups and communities whose experiences of migration might be explored within Key Stage 3 and Key Stage 4 lessons/units include the Vikings, Anglo-Saxons, Normans, Jews, Huguenots, Africans, Commonwealth workers and Eastern European migrants. The GCSE specifications additionally emphasise the importance of distinguishing between the experiences of asylum seekers, refugees and economic migrants.[2] Contemporary events make the nuanced teaching of migration even more important. Pupils ought to be equipped, for example, to situate recent debates about the settled status of Windrush migrants and Eastern European migrants (in light of Brexit) within a historical context. They also ought to understand the historical precedents and contexts according to which the present refugee crisis came into being.

This chapter therefore outlines a number of case studies that can be used to exemplify certain groups' or communities' experiences of migration. Several of these

---

1 Department for Education, *History Programmes of Study: Key Stage 3*, p. 5.
2 For example, see Pearson Education Limited, GCSE (9–1) *History: Specification content: Paper 1 Option 13, Migrants in Britain, c800–Present and Notting Hill, c1948–c1970* (March 2021). Available at: https://qualifications.pearson.com/content/dam/pdf/GCSE/History/2016/specification-and-sample-assessments/Pearson-Edexcel-GCSE-History-Migration-topic-final-draft.pdf.

might be featured within thematic migration units; others might serve to enrich the delivery of different topics, underlining the extent to which Elizabethan society, industrial Britain and/or the American West were founded upon the movement of different peoples. Seeking to complicate the picture presented of migrants and migration in contemporary society, the case studies acknowledge the complex reasons that have prompted migration, the experiences of migrants upon arrival in a foreign or strange environment and the longer-term consequences of migration – both for those who undertook the journeys, and for the societies and communities to which they migrated.

LICORICIA, THE MONEYLENDER OF WINCHESTER

> ● **Suggested enquiry:** How should we commemorate Licoricia of Winchester? (Significance)
>
> ● **Alternative enquiry:** How typical were the experiences of Licoricia of Winchester? (Similarity and difference)

Born in the early thirteenth century, Licoricia was a Jewish businesswoman who benefitted initially from the invitation extended to foreign-born Jewish money-lenders by William the Conqueror and subsequent Norman kings. In Norman and medieval England, the Christian Church ruled that Christians who lent money with interest were committing the sin of usury; therefore, only Jews were permitted to partake in this activity. Licoricia appears in the historical records from the 1230s onwards, lending money both independently and in association with other Jewish moneylenders. Her clients included King Henry III of England, who seems to have intervened on Licoricia's behalf when Licoricia was accused of withholding cus-tody of a rich heir's estate. Aside from her significance as a medieval woman who strove for financial independence, Licoricia represents an important case study in the experiences of Jewish people living in medieval England. Licoricia was subject to increased suspicion and persecution and was ultimately murdered in her house on Jewry Street, Winchester. The murder itself is likely to have been motivated less by antisemitic sentiment than by the prospect of financial gain, as a large amount of money was also stolen from Licoricia's house at the time of her murder. However, the fact that the three men indicted for the murder were never convicted probably reflects attitudes towards the status (or otherwise) of Jewish people liv-ing in England at the time.[3]

---

3 For a useful overview of Licoricia's story, see Hillary Waterman, 'Licoricia of Winchester, Jewish Widow and Medieval Financier', *JSTOR Daily* (28 October 2015). Available at: https://daily.jstor.org/licoricia-jewish-medieval-women-moneylenders/.

HOW SHOULD WE COMMEMORATE LICORICIA OF WINCHESTER? (SIGNIFICANCE)

A significance enquiry is a good way of exploring Licoricia's unique experiences, as well as underlining the ways in which Licoricia's life intersected with the broader narratives of anti-foreign sentiment in medieval England. There are numerous frameworks that can be used to judge historical significance, but in this case Ian Dawson's model works well: according to Dawson, a person or event might be considered significant if he/she/it changed events at the time they lived, affected many lives by improving them or making them worse, changed people's lives, had a lasting impact and represented a good or bad example of how to live and behave.[4] Providing pupils with a grid containing some, or all, of these criteria and then distributing clues relating to aspects of Licoricia's life, allows pupils to gather evidence about Licoricia's contemporary and continued significance.

Pupils might note, for example, that Licoricia fulfilled the criteria for having had a lasting impact through the funding she provided for Westminster Abbey to be rebuilt. They might also recognise Licoricia as a good example of how to live and behave through the support she provided for other Jews living in her community. Though Licoricia herself was murdered in 1277, Licoricia's son Benedict became the only Jewish guildsman in medieval England (and possibly anywhere else in Western Europe), meaning that he was permitted to own property and call himself a citizen of England. These rights were only possible for Benedict because of the work Licoricia had done to secure the family name.

In 2017, the Licoricia of Winchester Appeal was registered as a charity, and organisers outlined plans for the erection of a life-sized bronze statue of Licoricia in Winchester's Jewry Street, as well as for the production of educational materials to support schools in teaching about Licoricia's life. According to the charity's website, the project is intended to 'educate the public about Winchester's medieval Jewish community, its role in society and its royal connections, and to promote religious tolerance and understanding.'[5] Sharing the charity's plans with pupils is an effective way of concluding an enquiry into Licoricia and her significance.

---

4   For an example of this significance criteria in action, see Ian Dawson, *What is History? Year 7 Pupil's Book* (Glasgow: Hodder, 2003), p. 31. In this example, Dawson uses the criteria to help pupils assess the significance of Horatio Nelson.
5   See https://licoricia.org.

Discussion might be instigated on the extent to which commemorative projects like the erection of statues can indeed help to promote 'religious tolerance and the value of diversity in the community.'[6] Finally, pupils may be challenged to write a plaque to accompany the finished statue, including in their write-ups an account of Licoricia's significance as a medieval Jewish moneylender. This activity helps pupils to develop their ability to summarise information in a succinct manner, as they consider the proposed audience for their plaques.

Licoricia's experiences were neither typical nor representative of Jewish people's experiences in medieval England. Early in her life, Licoricia achieved a degree of acceptance and prosperity that would have been unrecognisable for the majority of Jewish men and women who had either migrated to England or who counted themselves amongst the first, second or even third-born generation of Jewish migrants. Bitterness and antisemitic feeling were to reach a climax in 1290, when Edward I submitted to public and political pressure and issued a decree for the expulsion of the Jews, signalling the start of a 350-year suspension of the Jewish right to live and work in England. However, Licoricia's story is worth telling by virtue of its uniqueness. Licoricia represents a woman of intelligence and ingenuity, who was able to exercise these talents for at least a portion of her life. Her experiences add substance to the story of diversity in medieval England.

KEY POINTS

- Licoricia of Winchester was a Jewish moneylender in medieval England.

- Norman and medieval monarchs invited Jewish moneylenders to settle in England, because Christians were forbidden from lending money with interest.

- Jewish men and women faced increasing persecution until Edward I issued a decree for their official expulsion in 1290.

- Licoricia achieved a degree of success unusual for Jewish people (especially Jewish women) of the time, and her story helps to underline the extent of diversity in medieval England.

---

6   See https://licoricia.org.

JAMIE MACPHERSON AND THE ROMANI GYPSIES OF EARLY MODERN SCOTLAND

- **Suggested enquiry:** Why was Jamie MacPherson hanged in 1700? (Causation)
- **Alternative enquiry:** What was the nature of Romani Gypsy migration in the early modern period? (Change and continuity/Similarity and difference)

It is difficult to trace the experiences of individual men and women who belonged to Romani Gypsy communities in early modern England and Scotland, although the story of Romani migration, settlement and expulsion is certainly one worth telling. In the sixteenth century it was thought that Romani people originated from Little Egypt (part of the Peloponnese peninsula in modern-day Greece) – hence the name 'Egyptians' or 'Gypsies'. However, it is now known that people of Romani heritage came from the Punjab region of northeast India. They migrated through Persia and had reached south-east Europe by the 1300s – and Western Europe by the following century. It is useful for pupils to chart the migration of Romani communities, and this can be done by providing them with a blank world map template and some brief captions relating to Romani migration patterns over time; pupils can draw arrows to plot some of the movements made by Romani people in different time periods as different groups encountered acceptance, opportunity or hostility. This activity underlines the scale of Romani migration, as well as the diverse and disparate nature of Romani communities. It also perhaps goes some way towards challenging stereotypes about the homogeneity of Romani Gypsy people.

Romani Gypsies who arrived in early modern England appear initially to have been welcomed, with their musical and fortune-telling skills highly prized by members of the local gentry, and even by the royal family. Still, these Gypsies carried papers with them certifying their status as itinerant pilgrims; clearly their safe passage through Europe was not guaranteed, if such paperwork was deemed necessary. Unfortunately, the more visible presence of Romani Gypsies in early modern England and Scotland combined with an upswing in vagrancy and in the minds of many contemporaries 'Gypsies' and 'vagrants' became interchangeable. It was in the context of a rising fear of vagrancy – as well as declining wages, population growth and poor harvests – that Jamie MacPherson and his mother experienced increasing hostility and resentment.

Jamie MacPherson was the son of a Gypsy woman and a Scottish landowner. Though MacPherson's father had acknowledged the birth of his son, he died when MacPherson was a child. MacPherson grew up with his mother's family, developing a reputation for swordsmanship and unusual physical strength. It is not clear how and why MacPherson's life descended into one of crime, although he seems to have been involved in instances of petty theft from a young age. MacPherson eventually became an outlaw, and his posse acquired local renown by virtue of the fact that they seem to have been heralded through the local markets by a piper. MacPherson's eventual capture was masterminded by the brilliantly named Lord Duff of Braco, and MacPherson was found guilty of the crimes of purse-cutting, theft and – most tellingly – being a Gypsy. MacPherson played a tune on his fiddle before accenting to his execution; the remains of the instrument (smashed by MacPherson in the moments before his death) are on display in a museum dedicated to the MacPherson clan in Newtonmore (in the Scottish Highlands).[7]

---

7   The National, 'A Parcel of Rogues: Jamie MacPherson – Making a Song and Dance over the Fate of Scotland's Robin Hood' (23 April 2016). Available at: https://www.thenational.scot/news/14864804.a-parcel-of-rogues-jamie-MacPherson-making-a-song-and-dance-over-the-fate-of-scotlands-robin-hood/. This article provides an overview of Jamie MacPherson's story.

WHY WAS JAMIE MACPHERSON HANGED IN 1700? (CAUSATION)

MacPherson's story reads like a folktale; there are elements that one would be forgiven for assuming were fictitious, and the events of his life have undoubtedly been embellished in the years since his death. Nevertheless, MacPherson's story can be used to deepen – and complicate – pupils' understanding of the experiences of Romani Gypsies in the early modern period.[8]

A causation enquiry entitled 'Why was Jamie MacPherson hanged in 1700?' might see pupils encounter evidence from MacPherson's life in a drip-feed manner, as they try to ascertain the causes (root, long-term, short-term and catalyst) for his death. This activity can be particularly engaging when it is undertaken as a class; guided by the teacher, pupils study each clue in turn and offer their inferences and hypotheses in real time, so that other pupils can benefit from the insights offered. Clues include extracts from contemporary Scottish and English laws (which criminalised the presence of Romani Gypsies in the early modern period), and lines from 'MacPherson's Rant' – a song thought to have been composed by MacPherson during his imprisonment, and since rewritten by Scottish bard Robert Burns.[9]

Ultimately, pupils ought to recognise that MacPherson's execution might be attributable in the short term to his criminal activities, but that the escalation in anti-Gypsy sentiment helps to provide important context for MacPherson's experiences. More broadly, the enquiry helps pupils to identify the historical precedents for modern prejudices against Gypsies, as well as providing opportunities to challenge some of the problematic assumptions made about them (sentiments which have, tragically, been used to justify wide-scale resettlement and elimination projects). Jamie MacPherson's criminal activities ought not to be downplayed; to do so would obscure the historical reality. Instead, it is important to emphasise the extent to which responses to MacPherson's crimes were shaped by anti-Gypsy sentiment – and, perhaps, to provide opportunities for parallels to be drawn with the more recent treatment of criminals from minority backgrounds.

---

8 Becky Taylor, *Another Darkness, Another Dawn: A History of Gypsies, Roma and Travellers* (London: Reaktion, 2014). This book provides a detailed overview of the experiences of Romani Gypsies and can be useful in gaining a broader picture of Romani migrations.

9 See https://www.scotslanguage.com/articles/node/id/449.

KEY POINTS

- Romani Gypsy migrants had arrived in Western Europe by the fourteenth century and appear initially to have been welcomed for their musical and fortune-telling skills.

- Jamie MacPherson was the son of a Romani Gypsy woman and a Scottish landowner.

- One of the crimes for which MacPherson was put to death was being a Gypsy, demonstrating the extent to which attitudes towards Gypsies had deteriorated.

- This enquiry helps pupils develop their causal explanations, as they apply terms like root, short-term, long-term and catalyst to explain the reasons for MacPherson's execution.

SACAGAWEA AND THE LEWIS AND CLARK EXPEDITION

> ● **Suggested enquiry:** How should Sacagawea's role on the Lewis and Clark Expedition be remembered? (Significance)
>
> ● **Alternative enquiry:** What can sources tell us about the life of Sacagawea? (Evidential understanding)

Sacagawea was born in around 1788 into a group of Lemhi Shoshone people, who lived in the modern-day north-west American state of Idaho. Conflict between the Shoshone and Hidatsa people resulted in Sacagawea (along with several other young Shoshone girls) being taken captive and, at the age of 13, Sacagawea was sold into marriage with a Quebec-born man called Toussaint Charbonneau. Charbonneau was a trapper, which meant that he was an expert in catching wild animals for food – and during the winter of 1804–1805 the explorers Meriweather Lewis and William Clark were seeking the help of trappers in guiding and/or interpreting for them on an expedition up the Missouri River. Charbonneau was hired for the job, largely due to the fact that his wife, Sacagawea, would be able to help the explorers communicate with Shoshone people they met along the way.

Two months after Sacagawea's baby had been born in February 1805, the expedition set off. During the challenging months ahead, it is clear from the explorers' diaries that Sacagawea made notable contributions to ensuring the expedition's – and indeed the explorers' – survival: she helped negotiate with Shoshone people for the purchase of horses and guides to take the explorers over the Rocky Mountains; she rescued precious items that had fallen out of a capsized boat; and, crucially, she made a number of recommendations relating to the route, saving the explorers time and safeguarding their well-being. Though the impact is hard to gauge, Sacagawea's presence on the expedition – as a woman, and as a representative of the Shoshone people – helped to ensure the explorers' safe passage; even William Clark noted in his diary 'as to our friendly intentions a woman with a party of men is a token of peace.'[10] With Sacagawea's help, the Lewis and Clark Expedition charted the land recently acquired for the United States in the Louisiana Purchase, reaching the Pacific Ocean as per the mission's objectives. Of course, the knowledge gained by the explorers also supported the American government in their push to encourage increased settlement in the west. This facilitated the increased colonisation of Indigenous American land, and the subdual of people for whom the land had been home for hundreds of years.

HOW SHOULD SACAGAWEA'S ROLE ON THE LEWIS AND CLARK EXPEDITION BE REMEMBERED? (SIGNIFICANCE)

The story of Sacagawea's role on the Lewis and Clark Expedition helps to develop pupils' understanding of America's founding story, and of settlers' conquest of the American West. It is a notable historical irony that the knowledge-gathering expedition upon which much of the later conquest of Indigenous Americans rested was only possible with the support of Sacagawea, who was herself of Indigenous American descent. It is important to underline the extent to which Sacagawea was coerced into participation on the Lewis and Clark Expedition; indeed, her whole life was strictly controlled from the point of her capture as a teenager. However, an enquiry centering upon Sacagawea's life and experiences should also emphasise her unique skills and knowledge, challenging false dichotomies between the 'pioneering, learned' American settlers and the 'backward, immutable' Indigenous Americans.

The enquiry might therefore begin with an examination of contemporary depictions of Sacagawea. These include the *Night at the Museum* films (in which Sacagawea was played by American actress Mizuo Peck)[11] and novels like *The Conquest: The True Story of Lewis and Clark* (written in 1902 by American suffragist Eva Emery Dye).[12] Dye's account is particularly problematic, given that it was

---

10 Meriwether Lewis, William Clark, et al., 13 October 1805 entry. In Gary Moulton (ed.), *The Journals of the Lewis & Clark Expedition* (Lincoln, NE: University of Nebraska Press / University of Nebraska-Lincoln Libraries-Electronic Text Center, 2005). Available at https://lewisandclarkjournals.unl.edu/item/lc.jrn.1805-10-13. The full diaries are available at: https://lewisandclarkjournals.unl.edu.
11 *Night at the Museum 1–3*, dir. Shawn Levy [film series] (20th Century Fox, 2006–2014).
12 Eva Emery Dye, *The Conquest: The True Story of Lewis and Clark* (Chicago: A.C. McClurg & Company, 1902).

founded less upon historical research and more upon Dye's efforts to elevate Sacagawea into a model for the feminist movement. Pupils could also look at some of the ways in which Sacagawea has been commemorated in statues and memorials, and on stamps. Although sometimes it is best to allow the real story to do the talking before flawed depictions of the individual are shared with pupils, in this case these depictions represent a good starting point – to which pupils can return as they develop their understanding of Sacagawea and her significance. To allow pupils to complete this activity, distribute large sheets of paper, with extracts from Dye's book, as well as portraits, stamps and other depictions. Ask pupils to annotate the extracts/images, noting down any problematic assumptions made about Sacagawea, and offering their own corrections/rewrites.

Next, pupils examine evidence relating to Sacagawea's life. Extracts from the explorers' diaries allow us to make inferences about Sacagawea's significance on the Lewis and Clark Expedition – even if Sacagawea's own voice is missing from these accounts. Finally, pupils ought to be in a position to dissect problematic depictions of Sacagawea. If pupils are given images of these depictions alongside short extracts from Eva Emery Dye's account, pupils can annotate and unpick these representations, perhaps rewriting/redrawing certain elements to lend them greater accuracy. This activity can help to give pupils a sense of empowerment, especially if the teacher continues to emphasise the misleading nature of existing representations. Encouraging pupils to dissect, critique and improve upon problematic claims and misappropriations of the past is surely one of our most important jobs as history teachers – and this enquiry equips pupils to do just this.

KEY POINTS

- Sacagawea was a Lemhi Shoshone woman whose local knowledge helped American explorers on their 1804–1805 expedition up the Missouri River.

- The expedition was part of a broader drive by settlers to expand America's borders westward.

- Sacagawea's image has been appropriated for various (sometimes problematic) purposes; suffragist campaigner Eva Emery Dye used Sacagawea as a model feminist.

- Sacagawea's story can be used to complicate pupils' understanding of Indigenous American passivity in the face of the American government's westward expansion.

GEORGE CATLIN AND THE MANNERS, CUSTOMS AND CONDITIONS OF THE NORTH AMERICAN INDIANS

- **Suggested enquiry:** How much can we learn from George Catlin about Indigenous American ways of life? (Evidential understanding)

- **Alternative enquiry:** How did new *scientific* ideas impact on attitudes towards Indigenous Americans in the nineteenth century? (Consequence/Change and continuity)

In the early 1840s, American explorer, artist, lawyer and entertainment impresario George Catlin organised for the exhibition of parties of Indigenous Americans on the British stage.[13] All three parties (two Ojibwe groups from the Lake Superior region of modern-day Canada, and one Iowa group from the Midwest region of America) had already been engaged by other travelling showmen and the *performers* had therefore become familiar, to some extent, with the wonder and excitement that greeted their appearance. The Indigenous Americans enacted the native customs which their audiences had come to expect. Amongst the rituals they play-acted was the scalp dance – a traditional practice which involved carving a cut around the crown of a defeated opponent's head, whereupon the scalp could be pulled off by the hair. As the Ojibwe and Iowa Americans performed, Catlin lectured on the cultural peculiarities of the different Indigenous Americans that he had come across during his travels. The Indigenous Americans even performed for Queen Victoria and her family. According to a correspondent from *The Times*, the Ojibwe 'war chief' was introduced by his native name (Pattana-quotto-weebe, which translated as 'swift-driving cloud'), and as the Ojibwe performed the 'war

---

13 For a biography of Catlin, see Benita Eisler, *The Red Man's Bones: George Catlin, Artist and Showman* (New York: W.W. Norton & Company, 2013).

dance' they wore 'the costume of their country', carrying such 'native' weapons as clubs, spears and tomahawks.[14] It must have been quite a spectacle to behold.

Though Catlin's own understanding of Indigenous American customs would have combined with the expectations of British audiences in determining the performances' format, the *real* Ojibwe and Iowa Americans were not stripped of all agency. Whilst the Indigenous Americans resided in England, British journalists were keen to present the visitors' interpretations of Britain and British people. Catlin encouraged this interest, including in his autobiographical writings the observations of the Ojibwe and Iowa Americans as they encountered aspects of British life. With Catlin and the journalists as their mouthpieces, the Indigenous Americans thereby acquired a level of subjecthood. They made astute, humourous and sometimes offensive observations, drawing the kinds of comparisons between their own and British society that would soon be institutionalised into the new science of anthropology (but often inverting these comparisons, so that the British seemed to be less *civilised*). When, for example, the Ojibwe took a walk through London's streets, they expressed surprise at the 'famishing creatures' (the homeless people) that populated London's streets. One of the Ojibwe Americans suggested that missionaries, instead of travelling to North America to work with the Indigenous Americans, ought to concern themselves with those dying on Britain's streets 'for want of food and knowledge'.[15] On another occasion, an Ojibwe American spotted a British man with 'a remarkably big nose' which, according to him, 'looked like a large potato (or *wapsapinnakan*).' An Ojibwe woman claimed that 'it was actually a *wapsapinnakan*, for she could distinctly see the little holes where the sprouts grow out.'[16]

---

14 The Glamorgan Monmouth and Brecon Gazette and Merthyr Guardian, 'The Ojibbeway Indians at Windsor Castle' (30 December 1843). Available at: https://newspapers.library.wales/view/3632965/3632967/.

15 Chambers' Edinburgh Journal, 'Savage Views of Civilisation' (24 June 1848), p. 408. Available at: https://archive.org/details/chambersedinburg9to10cham/page/408/mode/2up.

16 George Catlin, *Adventures of the Ojibbeway and Iowa Indians in England, France and Belgium, Being Notes of Eight Years' Travels and Residence in Europe with his North American Indian Collection* (London: published by author, 1852), p. 11.

HOW MUCH CAN WE LEARN FROM GEORGE CATLIN ABOUT INDIGENOUS AMERICAN WAYS OF LIFE? (EVIDENTIAL UNDERSTANDING)

I have used this enquiry as a way of introducing study of the American West at Key Stage 3, and the same could be done at Key Stage 4. The enquiry serves to highlight the extent to which all depictions of Indigenous Americans have been mediated through Western eyes – although it also offers an opportunity to approach a more authentic understanding of some aspects of Indigenous American ways of life, as the comments and interpretations of the Ojibwe Americans are placed at the forefront.

Pupils might begin by examining extracts from Catlin's diaries, letters and books, including comments made by the Ojibwe and Iowa Indians upon whom Catlin based his travelling show. Pupils can make inferences and identify evidence about different aspects of Indigenous American life, recording their findings in a grid; this information can be categorised according to whether it describes the daily life/ structure of Indigenous American society, methods of survival, beliefs about the land and nature or attitudes towards war.

Before responding to the enquiry question, it is interesting to share some of the famous depictions of Indigenous Americans with pupils, allowing them to assess the extent to which these depictions might be considered accurate.[17] Commenting on the usefulness of certain types of sources for a specific enquiry is a key skill that pupils need to develop at Key Stage 4. Provide pupils with a writing frame to support their conclusions here: *'The most important things that we can learn about Indigenous American life from Catlin's works are … . This is shown by … . However, there are certain aspects that we cannot learn, or which are obscured by Catlin and his writing … .'* Finally, pupils are asked to discuss the purpose for which Catlin exhibited the Indigenous Americans on stage. Catlin was purportedly concerned that the Indigenous Americans would soon 'disappear', and therefore wanted to produce a 'delineation of the living manners, customs, and character' of a 'truly

---

17 Bruce Watson, 'George Catlin's Obsession', *Smithsonian Magazine* (December 2002). Available at: https://www.smithsonianmag.com/arts-culture/george-catlins-obsession-72840046/. This article examines the extent to which Catlin's portraits of Indigenous Americans can be seen as exploitative.

lofty and noble race'.[18] This language can be unpicked, as can the extent to which Catlin's intentions might be considered morally justifiable.

KEY POINTS

- American writer and artist George Catlin engaged groups of Ojibwe and Iowa Americans as performers, organising for them to be exhibited on the British stage.

- Catlin sometimes allowed the Ojibwe and Iowa Americans a degree of agency, as he recorded their perceptions in his written works.

- The Ojibwe and Iowa Americans commented disparagingly on the extent of poverty they witnessed in Britain.

- Extracts from Catlin's account can be used to frame an overview enquiry on Indigenous American experiences during the period of westward expansion.

---

18 George Catlin, *Letters and Notes on the Manners, Customs and Conditions of the North American Indians* (London: Tosswill and Myers, 1841), p. 21.

A CAPTIVE GIRL: SARAH FORBES BONETTA

- **Suggested enquiry:** How typical was the story of Sarah Forbes Bonetta? (Significance)
- **Alternative enquiry:** To what extent did the experiences of Black migrants in Britain change during the eighteenth and nineteenth centuries? (Change and continuity)

Born in 1843 with the name Omoba Aina, Sarah Forbes Bonetta was from the village of Oke Odan, formerly part of the West African Oyo Empire (in modern-day Nigeria). In 1848, soldiers from the powerful neighbouring kingdom of Dahomey invaded Oke Odan, and Bonetta's parents – considered local royalty – were killed. Many other residents of Oke Odan were sold into slavery, and Bonetta was captured as a prize by the Dahomey victors. She became a child slave of the Dahomey court. Two years later, Royal Navy captain Frederick Forbes arrived on a British diplomatic mission, apparently attempting to persuade the King of Dahomey to cease participation in the slave trade. As part of the traditional exchange of gifts, Forbes was given the 'captive girl' (Forbes thereby participated to some extent in the trade to which he professedly objected). Forbes renamed the 7-year-old 'Sarah Forbes Bonetta' in tribute to himself and his ship, the HMS *Bonetta*, and transported her back to Britain. Bonetta was to be raised as Queen Victoria's goddaughter, and she was – ostensibly at least – to enjoy all of the privileges of an upper-class English upbringing.[19]

Bonetta's story helps to exemplify one of the key themes in GCSE migration units: namely, the experiences of migrants to Britain during the nineteenth century. Bonetta was treated as an object of fascination and her *exoticism* helped to ensure that the intimate details of her life were known to both press and public in the gossip-hungry Victorian age. It is clear that Bonetta benefitted from educational opportunities and access to significant material riches, but the physical and

---

19 English Heritage, 'Sarah Forbes Bonetta, Queen Victoria's African Protégée' (n.d.). Available at: https://www.english-heritage.org.uk/visit/places/osborne/history-and-stories/sarah-forbes-bonetta/.

emotional costs were high. Bonetta was virtually forced into marriage, with her patron (Queen Victoria) endorsing the match; Bonetta herself wrote 'Others would say, "He is a good man & you will soon learn to love him." That, I believe, I could never do.' Her wedding was a public spectacle designed to emphasise her and her new husband's African heritage, with the wedding party formed of 'white ladies with African gentlemen, and African ladies with white gentlemen.' Finally, Bonetta's married life was blighted by illness and she died from tuberculosis at the age of just 37.[20]

HOW TYPICAL WAS THE STORY OF SARAH FORBES BONETTA? (SIGNIFICANCE)

This significance enquiry might first help pupils to recall key dates and events relating to Britain's changing relationship with Africa. Pupils need to be aware that British interest in the continent had by no means dissipated after the formal abolition of the slave trade in 1833; though Bonetta's story predates the Scramble for Africa, the process of establishing British trading posts along the West African coast was well under way by the 1840s, as was the attempt by various missionary societies to rid Africans of their *heathenistic* tendencies. Having developed an understanding of the broader context, pupils might then read a summary of Bonetta's story. As they read, pupils could highlight (using three different colours) evidence of Bonetta's reception in Britain: in one colour, they can highlight evidence of Bonetta being treated with warmth; in a second colour, evidence of Bonetta being treated with curiosity; and in a third colour, evidence of Bonetta being treated with hostility or disrespect. This activity encourages pupils to recognise that the experiences of migrants were rarely consistent. Pupils might note, for example, the strictness with which Bonetta's life was controlled; her childhood ill health was attributed to the British climate, and she was sent to Sierra Leone to become a missionary. Bonetta was treated as different or foreign, as though her physical being was fundamentally incompatible with the life of a true English lady. Pupils might also be guided to identify some of the language of racial inferiority that ran through newspaper reports relating to Bonetta; one journalist commented that her wedding represented the union of 'two Anglicised, wealthy,

---

20 English Heritage, 'Sarah Forbes Bonetta, Queen Victoria's African Protégée'.

well-connected Africans', the success of which could be attributed to 'philanthropists and the missionary … over the prejudices of pride and blood.'[21]

Next, pupils might consider the extent to which Bonetta's experiences were typical of Black migrants in Britain during the eighteenth and nineteenth centuries, by examining the experiences of individuals such as Mary Seacole and Ignatius Sancho. Seacole was a nurse and businesswoman who set up a hospital during the Crimean War, and Sancho was an abolitionist who was famous for being the first person of African descent to vote in a British general election. The contexts in which Bonetta, Seacole and Sancho lived were very different; neither Seacole nor Sancho had the benefit of royal patronage, and Sancho was born into slavery. Nevertheless, asking pupils to identify evidence of warmth, curiosity and hostility in responses to these three migrants helps to underline the divergent, changeable nature of their reception in Britain. Finally, pupils might begin to account for some of these responses by evaluating the possible impact of events from the time, including the campaign for abolition, the publication of evolutionary tracts (which held non-Whites to be less advanced, both physically and morally), and the increasing penchant for curiosities on the Victorian stage.

The enquiry underlines the extent to which migrants' experiences were contingent upon the context. It was easier to infantilise and subjugate Black migrants, for example, when science had provided apparent evidence of their physical and intellectual retardation. Bonetta's story is unique, but it helps to shed light on the lives of men and women whose experiences in nineteenth-century British society were rather more equivocal than they might reasonably have expected.

KEY POINTS

- Sarah Forbes Bonetta was born in West Africa and was taken to Britain as a young girl when she was gifted to the Royal Navy captain Frederick Forbes.

- Bonetta was raised as Queen Victoria's goddaughter.

- Although Bonetta's status conferred a number of material benefits, her life was strictly controlled.

---

21 Megan Orr, 'Ladylike in the Extreme: The Propagandism of Sarah Forbes Bonetta, Britain's 'African Princess'' (2 December 2021). Available at: https://scholarsarchive.byu.edu/cgi/viewcontent. cgi?article=1348&context=studentpub.

- By examining the varying responses to Bonetta in Britain, pupils can be guided to recognise the diverse nature of migrants' experiences in the nineteenth century.

BEYOND A BOUNDARY: C. L. R. JAMES

- **Suggested enquiry:** What impact did C. L. R. James have on Pan-African independence movements in the twentieth century? (Significance)

- **Alternative enquiry:** How typical were C. L. R. James' experiences of migration to Britain in the twentieth century? (Change and continuity)

In the preface to his autobiographical book *Beyond a Boundary* (1963), the Marxist writer C. L. R. James explained the intellectual impact of his own experiences of migration: 'If the ideas originated in the West Indies it was only in England and in English life and history that I was able to track them down and test them. To establish his own identity, Caliban, after three centuries, must himself pioneer into regions Caesar never knew.'[22] James went on to recount some of the key events of his life, touching on the wider issues of nationality, class and colonialism – and examining all of this through the prism of cricket. From behind the veil of sporting commentary, James was able to make several penetrating – and highly disparaging – comments about the continued impact of colonialism in places like Britain: 'There are people who, having enjoyed the profits and privileges of racialism for most of a lifetime, now that racialism is under fire and in retreat, profess a lofty scorn for it and are terribly pained when you so much as refer to it in any shape or form. Their means have changed, not their ends, which are the same as they always were, to exploit racialism for their own comfort and convenience.' The 'profits and privileges' to which James referred were of course wealth and status, and Britain's achievement of these ends relied upon the 'exploitation of common labour' – with cricket being appropriated as a means of keeping *civilised* working-class society in check.[23]

James was one of many thousands of West Indians who migrated to Britain in the twentieth century, although his arrival predated the Windrush generation's famous homecoming of the 1950s and 1960s (many of whom arrived in the *mother*

---

22 C. L. R. James, *Beyond a Boundary* (London: Yellow Jersey Press, 2005), Preface.
23 James, *Beyond a Boundary*, p. 78.

country in answer to calls for cheap labour after the Second World War). Born in Trinidad in 1901, James worked as a teacher on the British Crown colony island before his friend – the West Indian cricketer Learie Constantine – requested James' help in writing his autobiography. James arrived in Lancashire in 1932 and, after completing his work on Constantine's manuscript, he took a job as a cricket correspondent for a British newspaper. It was at this point that James nursed his passion for Marxism, and he began to give speeches and write political tracts urging support for Pan-African independence movements. James believed that class struggle lay at the heart of progress in Caribbean liberation. In his support for racial equality and Black independence movements, James' ideas overlapped with those of the famous Jamaican migrant Dr Harold Moody, whose establishment of the League of Coloured Peoples proved so influential.

James went on an international lecture tour, speaking in various American cities about the 'Twilight of the British Empire' and 'The Negro People and World Imperialism';[24] in Mexico he met Leon Trotsky and discussed the anticipated future uprising of the Pan-African movement. James was interned as a communist in America in 1953 but continued to agitate for African and Caribbean independence until he died in London in 1989.

WHAT IMPACT DID C. L. R. JAMES HAVE ON PAN-AFRICAN INDEPENDENCE MOVEMENTS IN THE TWENTIETH CENTURY? (SIGNIFICANCE)

Examining the Pan-African independence movement allows us to emphasise the agency and dynamism of migrants like C. L. R. James. This enquiry might therefore begin by spotlighting James' political and intellectual roots, encouraging pupils to study extracts from James' own writings. Then, pupils could plot the intersections between James' career and the growth of the Pan-African independence movement, identifying ways in which James shaped the movement (and was, in turn, shaped *by* the movement). A linking diagram might help pupils conceptualise some of these connections. Provide pupils with a sheet containing a number of words/phrases in separate bubbles; pupils are challenged to identify links

---

24 Both speeches are discussed in Scott McLemee (ed.), *C. L. R. James on the 'Negro Question'* (Jackson, MS: University Press of Mississippi, 1996), pp. xii–xiii.

between two or more of the bubbles. For example, some of the bubbles relating to James might read *Twilight of British Empire*, *Communism* and *Exploitation of ordinary people*, whilst some of the bubbles relating to wider events might include *1917 Russian Revolution*, *1919 race riots* and *Colonial decline.*

For me, it is important to dwell upon terms such as revolt, revolution and independence (all of which represent first-order or substantive concepts). Our teaching should provide opportunities for tracing these events' recurrence in different time periods – and for identifying ways in which the context affected their particular manifestations. Therefore, situating Pan-Africanism within the context of the early twentieth century (and noting, for example, the movement's links with the 1917 Russian Revolution and the 1919 race riots in the USA) helps pupils to make sense of the vociferous calls for African independence. Doing so also makes it easier for pupils to understand why the movement was greeted with such contempt, as contemporaries grappled with numerous perceived threats to the political and social order.

Pan-Africanism did not develop within a vacuum; calls for African independence could only have emerged as a corollary of earlier events, such as the rise and decline of the slave trade, the expansion of colonial influence, and the migration and displacement of different peoples in pre- and post-war society. C. L. R. James' story helps to exemplify the impact that individuals could have on the development of these global narratives – but also the extent to which individual lives were shaped by broader forces that remained firmly outside of their own control.

KEY POINTS

- C. L. R. James was a Trinidadian who migrated to Britain during the 1930s. He had a significant impact on the development of Pan-African independence movements.

- James' ideas were influenced by events like the 1917 Russian Revolution and the 1919 race riots in America.

- Responses to Pan-Africanism were impacted by wider global events. Some people identified Pan-Africanism as a threat to political and social stability.

- James' experiences help to add flavour to the story of decolonisation and its various manifestations in the twentieth century.

THE MOTHER OF CARIBBEAN CARNIVAL IN BRITAIN: CLAUDIA JONES

- **Suggested enquiry:** Was Britain really the wicked stepmother to African-Caribbean migrants like Claudia Jones? (Interpretations)

- **Alternative enquiry:** What can we learn from Claudia Jones about Black activism amongst the Windrush generation? (Significance/Consequence)

Claudia Jones was born on the Caribbean island of Trinidad in 1915. At the age of 9 she migrated to New York as her parents sought new opportunities for work. Although Jones graduated from high school, her immigrant status limited the career choices open to her. Whilst working in a launderette, she joined the Young Communist League (a youth organisation committed to the study of Marx's works) and joined the fight to improve the circumstances of Black men and women, as well as members of the working classes. In an article entitled 'An End to the Neglect of the Problems of the Negro Woman!' (1949), Jones wrote, 'The bourgeoisie is fearful of the militancy of the Negro woman, and for good reason. The capitalists know ... that once Negro women undertake action, the militancy of the whole Negro people, and thus of the anti-imperialist coalition, is greatly enhanced.'[25] Jones' activities eventually got her in trouble with the law and she was threatened with deportation to Trinidad. Following a prison term, she was refused entry to Trinidad and instead offered the opportunity to reside in Britain. Jones arrived in London in 1955, at a time when the Caribbean community in Britain had swelled following the arrival of HMT *Empire Windrush* in 1948.

In 1958, Jones set up a newspaper called the *West Indian Gazette*, hoping to give voice to the Black British community in London. Articles described the experiences of African and African-Caribbean migrants in Britain; they also reported on

---

25 Claudia Jones, 'An End to the Neglect of the Problems of the Negro Woman!' (New York: National Women's Commission, 1949), p. 3. Available at: https://palmm.digital.flvc.org/islandora/object/ucf%3A4865.

developments in African independence movements, and in the American Civil Rights movement. Jones claimed that the newspaper served as a 'catalyst', heightening people's awareness of the social, economic and political issues affecting Black British communities.[26] However, just four months after the launch of the *West Indian Gazette*, the Notting Hill riots took place – highlighting the hostility that London's black population continued to face. Deciding that the Black British community needed to move past the events of the Notting Hill riots, Jones helped to organise a 'Caribbean Carnival'. Further carnival events were organised during the 1960s, and the Notting Hill Carnival was born. The event is considered instrumental in highlighting – and consolidating – the cultural heritage of African Caribbean people living in Notting Hill and beyond.

WAS BRITAIN REALLY THE WICKED STEPMOTHER TO AFRICAN-CARIBBEAN MIGRANTS LIKE CLAUDIA JONES? (INTERPRETATIONS)

In her book *Mother Country: Real Stories of the Windrush Children* (2018), journalist Charlie Brinkhurst-Cuff noted that although Britain was known as the 'mother country' or the 'motherland' by its colonial subjects, it was far from 'maternal' for most Caribbean migrants: 'motherhood in our society still represents nurture and life, but the UK was a wicked stepmother of the Cinderella variety to those brave enough to make the journey.'[27] This is an interesting interpretation around which to base the enquiry, which aims to foreground the prejudices faced by newcomers in the mid-twentieth century – as well as celebrating the lasting impact that African-Caribbean migrants had on British life and culture.

The enquiry might therefore see pupils examine a range of sources relating to Jones' experiences, allowing them to build a nuanced – and personalised – picture of Windrush migrants' experiences. Pupils can read extracts from some of Jones' most famous articles and opinion pieces, and they can examine her role in helping to develop Black activism in Britain and beyond. Pupils' final responses might take

---

26 Carole Boyce Davies, *Left of Karl Marx: The Political Life of Black Communist Claudia Jones* (Durham: Duke University Press, 2008), p. 88.

27 Charlie Brinkhurst-Cuff, *Mother Country: Real Stories of the Windrush Children* (London: Headline Publishing Group, 2018), Introduction.

the form of an extended piece of writing – or alternatively, they might be given a more creative task. In 2020, Jones was the subject of a Google Doodle; pupils might be challenged to develop this method of commemoration, drawing upon their knowledge of Jones' contributions to Black British life and culture.

Claudia Jones' story might additionally be used to prompt discussion about the recent controversies surrounding the settled status of Windrush migrants. In April 2018, the government was forced to apologise when the children of Windrush-generation migrants were threatened with deportation, following claims that a lack of official paperwork invalidated their right to reside in Britain. An enquiry in March 2020 blamed the scandal upon 'a culture of disbelief and carelessness' within the Home Office, and a compensation scheme was introduced, along with official channels through which second-generation migrants could apply for proof to live and work in Britain.[28] However, the episode raised important questions about the systems that are in place to support first and second-generation migrants living in Britain – and, indeed, about the status which ought to be accorded to migrants (when does a migrant become simply a citizen?). It would be instructive, therefore, for pupils to conclude their study of Claudia Jones with an examination of the Windrush scandal, using their knowledge of African-Caribbean migrants' experiences to compose a set of recommendations to help guide the responses of the British government today.

KEY POINTS

- Claudia Jones migrated from Trinidad (via the USA) to Britain during the 1950s.

- In London, Jones launched the *West Indian Gazette* as a mouthpiece for local African and African-Caribbean communities, and she was instrumental in establishing the Notting Hill Carnival as a celebration of African-Caribbean culture.

- Jones had a mobilising influence on Black British activists.

- Jones' story helps add nuance to pupils' understanding of migrants' experiences in twentieth-century Britain.

---

28 Wendy Williams, *Windrush Lessons Learned Review* (March 2020), p. 7. Ref: ISBN 978-1-5286-1779-6. Available at: https://assets.publishing.service.gov.uk/government/uploads/system/uploads/attachment_data/file/876336/6.5577_HO_Windrush_Lessons_Learned_Review_LoResFinal.pdf.

Grace O'Malley, see page 70.

Chapter 3

POWER AND POLITICS (BRITAIN)

INTRODUCTION

Power is a weighty term and, like many of the first-order concepts around which our history curricula are shaped, it requires a good deal of unpacking in order for pupils to appreciate its complexity – as well as its changing application and relevance in different contexts.

It is likely that pupils have developed some conception of power in a British context by the time they enter Key Stage 3. At Key Stage 2, the national curriculum stipulates that pupils learn about various powerful individuals and institutions such as the Roman Empire and emperors, Anglo-Saxon and Viking invaders, and English kings and queens; pupils might also explore 'the changing power of monarchs using case studies such as John, Anne and Victoria', as well as the political, legal and cultural legacies of individuals in positions of authority.[1] The *History Programmes of Study: Key Stage 3* document requires teachers to build on this work by delivering lessons focused on various manifestations of 'political power', with examples including 'party politics, extension of the franchise and social reform'. Teachers are also advised to examine 'the changing nature of political power in Britain' as a means by which to consolidate pupils' chronological awareness.[2] There is a danger, however, in dedicating schemes of work to a rather narrowly defined conception of power (namely, one that emphasises the dominance and authority of monarchs, politicians and – it must be said – men) that pupils come to view as a rather exclusive (and exclusionist) tool which is claimed by only a certain, privileged few. It is concerning, too, that pupils' focus might be directed only towards the powerful when there is a great deal to be learnt from a study of the supposedly powerless; the disenfranchised, outcast and persecuted, or those who have fallen foul of the institutions of power in consequence of class, rank, gender or circumstance.

The case studies in this section focus on individuals in a British context who have challenged perceived injustices or acted on behalf of the overlooked and oppressed. They also explore the stories of men and women we might perceive to have been lacking in power, because the experiences of these individuals can tell

1   Department for Education, *History Programmes of Study: Key Stages 1 and 2* (2013). Ref: DFE-00173-2013, p. 5. Available at: https://assets.publishing.service.gov.uk/government/uploads/system/uploads/attachment_data/file/239035/PRIMARY_national_curriculum_-_History.pdf.
2   Department for Education, *History Programmes of Study: Key Stage 3*, pp. 4–5.

us a good deal about the impact of decisions made by those in positions of authority – and, indeed, about the lived experiences of ordinary people in the past. It is likely that their stories might feature within broader schemes of work, focused, for example, on the reign of Elizabeth I, the English Civil War or the political and social reforms of the nineteenth century. However, by choosing to employ the suggested enquiries as starting points – rather than adjuncts – for the study of these topics, traditional notions of power (as top-down, uncompromising and unassailable) are disrupted, and pupils are encouraged to view power as a much less monolithic concept.

WALTER HUNGERFORD AND THE 'ACTE FOR THE PUNISHMENT OF THE VICE OF BUGGERIE'

- **Suggested enquiry:** Why was Tudor landowner and sheriff Walter Hungerford executed in 1540? (Causation)
- **Alternative enquiry:** What can we learn from Walter Hungerford's case about attitudes towards sexuality in the early modern period? (Significance)

On 28 July 1540, Walter Hungerford – Lord Hungerford of Heytesbury and friend of Thomas Cromwell (one of Henry VIII's chief advisers) – was sent to his death on Tower Hill. This particular spot had recently seen the execution of Anne Boleyn, the second wife of Henry VIII, and Thomas More, an opponent of Henry's Protestant Reformation – so Hungerford was in revered company. However, the crime for which Hungerford faced the executioner's axe was very different from those committed by Henry VIII's other victims. Hungerford was accused and convicted of the crime of buggery (homosexuality), and he was the first person in England to fall foul of the Buggery Act (the 'Acte for the punishment of the vice of Buggerie') passed just seven years earlier in 1533.[3]

Born in 1503, Walter Hungerford inherited his father's considerable estate at the age of 19 and became esquire of the body (personal attendant) to Henry VIII. Hungerford married three times, and the father of his third wife Elizabeth (John Hussey) introduced Hungerford to Thomas Cromwell, a prominent member of Henry's Privy Council who was seeking to obtain a divorce on Henry's behalf from Catherine of Aragon. Hungerford requested that Cromwell appoint him sheriff of Wiltshire – a position which would see Hungerford preside over law and order in

---

3 English Heritage, 'Walter Hungerford and the "Buggery Act"' (n.d.). Available at: https://www.english-heritage.org.uk/learn/histories/lgbtq-history/walter-hungerford-and-the-buggery-act/.

the county – and Hungerford's request was granted. Hungerford was later rewarded for his work when Cromwell recommended his appointment to the title of lord.

In 1536, Hungerford's wife Elizabeth sent a letter to Cromwell, informing him of Hungerford's ill treatment of her. She said that he had locked her in a tower at their family home for three or four years, and had 'once or twice heretofore poisoned me'. Significantly, she declared that if Cromwell did not help her to obtain a divorce, she 'may sooner object such matters against him [Hungerford] with many other detestable and urgent causes, than he can against me, if I would express them, as he well knoweth.'[4] Within this claim it is possible to detect the implication that Hungerford was homosexual – and that he might have been embarrassed (or worse) if Elizabeth's accusations were allowed to surface. However, Cromwell seems at this point to have ignored the letter.

Four years later, Elizabeth's accusations assumed renewed importance. Hungerford's chaplain was accused of involvement in the 1536 revolt known as the Pilgrimage of Grace (a protest against Henry's break with Rome), and Hungerford was implicated in this; he was also accused of using witchcraft to determine how long Henry would live. Finally, Hungerford was accused of the 'detestable vice and sin of buggery' – or of having engaged in homosexual acts with his servants.[5] Elizabeth's earlier claims seemed to carry new weight and Hungerford was accused – and found guilty – of the crimes of treason, witchcraft and buggery. He was executed on the same day as his former friend and master Thomas Cromwell, whose own fortunes had declined when he recommended that Henry marry Anne of Cleves on the strength of a misleading portrait.

4   English Heritage, 'Walter Hungerford and the 'Buggery Act''.
5   English Heritage, 'Walter Hungerford and the 'Buggery Act''.

WHY WAS TUDOR LANDOWNER AND SHERIFF WALTER HUNGERFORD EXECUTED IN 1540? (CAUSATION)

This causation enquiry allows pupils to explore the complex reasons behind Hungerford's fall from favour – and to consider the ways in which accusations of immorality could be used to eliminate troublesome or threatening individuals.[6] Pupils could examine clues in a drip-feed manner, using evidence to reach and refine their hypotheses in relation to the enquiry question. Having examined a range of clues, they should be in a position to explain the ways in which root, underlying, short-term and long-term causes coincided to ensure that Hungerford's position had definitively fallen by the beginning of 1540.

Once pupils have explored Hungerford's heady rise to power, his friendship with the ill-fated but morally steadfast Thomas Cromwell, and his links to the Pilgrimage of Grace (one of the most destabilising events in Henry's reign), it becomes clear that Hungerford's homosexuality was not the sole – nor perhaps even the most important – reason for his execution in 1540. The passing of the Buggery Act in 1533 would seem to provide evidence of Henry's desire to transmute the issue of sexual morality from ecclesiastical to state control – and ought, therefore, to be situated within the context of the English Reformation, which saw Henry wrest control of a staggering number of rights and responsibilities from the hands of the church. At this point, it is useful to ask pupils to explain why some of the following events might have been so significant (and/or destabilising): Henry's break with Rome and the annulment of his marriage to Catherine of Aragon in 1533, the Dissolution of the Monasteries after 1536, the annulment of Henry's marriage to Anne Boleyn (and her execution) in 1536 and the Pilgrimage of Grace in 1536–1537.

Ultimately, Hungerford's power proved to be rather insubstantial; though he had spent his entire life campaigning for political advancement, Henry was able to disempower Hungerford seemingly on a whim. However, Hungerford's story does expose some of the insecurities that lay at the heart of Henry's own government. Often presumed to be monolithic and indomitable, Henry's rule had clearly been

---

6   For further examples see Alan Bray, *Homosexuality in Renaissance England* (New York: Columbia University Press, 1982). This book compares images of homosexuality in Renaissance literature with the experiences of real men.

built on rather shaky ground. Hungerford's transgression of accepted social and sexual norms was seized upon by Henry and his advisers, allowing them to eliminate one of many threats identified during a period of real turbulence and uncertainty for the Tudor monarchy.

KEY POINTS

- Walter Hungerford was a personal attendant to Henry VIII. His friendship with Thomas Cromwell saw him assume responsibility for law and order in Wiltshire.

- Hungerford's third wife, Elizabeth, accused him of ill treatment and her letters to Cromwell indicate that Hungerford might have been homosexual.

- Hungerford was eventually found guilty of the crime of buggery and executed in 1540.

- Accusations of sexual immorality could be used to eliminate threats to the monarch's power and authority.

THE LIFE, DEATH AND AFTERLIFE OF AMY DUDLEY

- **Suggested enquiry:** Should the Tate museum display the painting *Amy Robsart*? (Significance)

- **Alternative enquiry:** What can we learn from Amy Dudley about life for women in Tudor England? (Similarity and difference)

In perhaps her most famous depiction, Tudor heiress and wife of Robert Dudley (one of Queen Elizabeth I's favourites) is shown sprawled at the bottom of a stair-case, her life having been extinguished by the two shady figures who watch on – somewhat warily – from a few steps above. Dudley is clothed in an ivory-coloured dress and shawl, which serve to accentuate her pitiful figure against the gloom of her surroundings – and, perhaps, to underline her youth and innocence. With no visible evidence of the violence that has been wrought upon her, Dudley appears peaceful in repose: a sleeping beauty rather than the battered victim of domestic abuse.

William Frederick Yeames' 1877 painting, *Amy Robsart*, depicts Dudley as a rather romantic victim; the painting is almost Pre-Raphaelite in style.[7] It is a rather one-dimensional representation of a woman whose death is already seen by many as the most important aspect of her life. However, in this enquiry pupils are encouraged to recognise Dudley's wider significance as a woman of wealth and rank during the period. Dudley's story can tell us a great deal about the experiences of women in Tudor England, providing a corrective to the traditional focus on Elizabeth and her (male) courtiers. The enquiry also offers an introduction to art history, as pupils are empowered to comment in sophisticated ways on the successes and failings of Yeames' artistic rendering of Dudley – and to suggest alternative ways in which her story might be interpreted and represented.

---

7   See https://www.tate.org.uk/art/artworks/yeames-amy-robsart-n01609.

Born in 1532, Amy Dudley was the only child of a wealthy landowner and she grew up at Stanfield Hall in Norfolk. At the age of 17 she married Robert Dudley and, according to a letter later written by Elizabeth I's chief advisor, Robert Cecil, it was a 'carnal marriage' (essentially a love match). At the time of the marriage, Robert Dudley's father – the Earl of Warwick – was probably the most powerful man in England, serving as King Edward VI's lord protector. However, when Edward died the Earl of Warwick made an unsuccessful attempt to install Lady Jane Grey onto the throne and, in consequence, Robert Dudley – as the earl's son – was imprisoned in the Tower of London. After his release, the couple moved to Amy's ancestral home and once Elizabeth ascended to the throne, Robert Dudley began to attend court much more regularly.[8]

The nature of the sources makes it difficult for us to know what happened next. Those wishing to discredit Dudley claimed that he was trying to poison his wife; others said that he planned to divorce Amy so that he was free to marry Elizabeth. There is some evidence that Amy was unwell at home whilst Dudley enjoyed Elizabeth's favour at court. In September 1560, Amy was found dead at the foot of a staircase at her home. Dudley was told of his wife's death by a messenger, and he immediately ordered an inquest. There were rumours that Amy might have committed suicide, although the final verdict was that the death had been accidental.[9] Though, of course, Elizabeth and Robert Dudley never married, the two remained close until Dudley's death in 1588.

SHOULD THE TATE MUSEUM DISPLAY THE PAINTING *AMY ROBSART*? (SIGNIFICANCE)

This enquiry might see pupils examine evidence relating to Amy Dudley's life, before developing their understanding of life for women in Tudor England; ultimately, pupils ought to be able to describe some of the ways in which Dudley's life is (and is not) instructive about – or typical of – life for women in the period. They can study Yeames' 1877 painting, adding annotations relating to some of the ways in which the piece might be considered problematic or misleading, given our

---

8 Christine Hartweg, *Amy Robsart: A Life and its End* (Scotts Valley: CreateSpace Independent Publishing Platform, 2017) p. 13. This book provides a short overview of the life of Amy Dudley, although it devotes most attention to the circumstances surrounding her death.

9 See https://www.nationalarchives.gov.uk/education/resources/elizabeth-monarchy/coroners-report/.

understanding of Amy's life (and death). Finally, pupils can write their conclusions in the form of a letter to the Tate museum, explaining whether the painting deserves to be displayed – and, if so, how it should be captioned in order to educate modern audiences about Amy Dudley and her significance.

Like countless women of Tudor England, Amy Dudley's life has been reduced and caricatured by the processes of history – and she has come to be defined by the men whose whims and desires did so much to shape her experiences in life. Lucy Moss and Toby Marlow's brilliant musical *Six* offers an important example of the ways in which we might rehabilitate these women; focusing on Henry's VIII's wives, it lingers upon the idea of possibility, celebrating some of the lives that women like Katherine Howard and Catherine Parr might have lived, if it were not for Henry's vain capriciousness.[10] This 'what if ... ' history is not only engaging but extremely important, and can be explored with creative results in the case of Amy Dudley, allowing pupils to imaginatively reconstruct Dudley's life, had it not been subsumed by the will of her more powerful and *significant* husband.

KEY POINTS

- Amy Dudley (née Robsart) was the wife of Robert Dudley, one of Queen Elizabeth I's favourites.

- Although the marriage appears initially to have been a love match, Robert distanced himself from Amy as he became closer to Elizabeth.

- Amy Dudley died at home in 1560 and the circumstances surrounding her death were controversial.

- Artistic renderings portray Amy Dudley as a helpless (and rather romantic) victim; this enquiry sees pupils rehabilitate her reputation.

---

10 *Six*, written and dir. by Toby Marlow and Lucy Moss [musical] (first performed 2017).

THE PIRATE QUEEN OF IRELAND: GRACE O'MALLEY

- **Suggested enquiry:** Why was the 1593 meeting between Elizabeth I and Grace O'Malley so significant? (Significance)

- **Alternative enquiry:** What can we learn from Grace O'Malley about sixteenth-century Ireland? (Change and continuity)

In an article on the Royal Museums Greenwich website, Grace O'Malley is granted the epithet 'one of the most famous pirates of all time', and the author claims that O'Malley is still today remembered as 'the pirate queen of Ireland'.[11] However, the term *pirate* – with its connotations of swashbuckling lawlessness – seems to do O'Malley something of a disservice. O'Malley was a landowner, reportedly owning around 1,000 cattle and horses, as well as a politician and negotiator; she organised a landmark meeting with Elizabeth I in 1593, when the English queen's representatives captured her sons as part of an attempt to quash a rebellion by the Irish lords. O'Malley also used her sailing prowess to help advance political and personal aims. In one instance, she led a charge on MacMahon Castle in Blacksod Bay (on the west coast of Ireland), seeking revenge for the murder of her lover. Unsurprisingly, O'Malley's life has been subject to significant revision and reinterpretation by folktales, plays, songs and books, but her story is worthy of study in the context of early modern gender relations. Her iconic meeting with Queen Elizabeth also serves as a useful case study in the changing relationship between England and Ireland in the late sixteenth century.

---

11 Royal Museums Greenwich, 'Grace O'Malley: The Pirate Queen of Ireland'. Available at: https://www.rmg.co.uk/stories/topics/grace-o-malley-irish-female-pirate. For an overview of Grace O'Malley's life, see Anne Chambers, *Grace O'Malley: The Biography of Ireland's Pirate Queen 1530–1603* (Dublin: Gill Books, 2018).

WHY WAS THE 1593 MEETING BETWEEN ELIZABETH I AND GRACE O'MALLEY SO SIGNIFICANT? (SIGNIFICANCE)

This enquiry is well situated within the study of Elizabethan England at Key Stages 3, 4 and 5. GCSE and A level specifications require pupils to develop an understanding of the manifestations of power and authority under Tudor government, and O'Malley's story provides an opportunity to examine some of the ways in which Elizabeth attempted to secure power in Ireland – although O'Malley's influence and authority ought not to be underestimated. I try to avoid uncontextualised use of words like *clan* and *tribe* because they can often connote backwardness and barbarism, but in this case it is important to paint a picture of O'Malley as the leader of the O'Malley (or Ó Máille) clan in western Ireland – and it is important, too, that pupils understand the meanings and significance of the clan system in early modern Ireland. O'Malley was heavily involved in the processes of wealth and land consolidation, making and breaking strategic alliances and protecting her lands against foreign encroachment. In meeting with Elizabeth in 1593, O'Malley was essentially petitioning Elizabeth for the removal of Richard Bingham – the English governor in Ireland and the man responsible for imprisoning O'Malley's sons. It is a sign of Elizabeth's respect for O'Malley that she ultimately agreed to unseat Bingham, and to confirm the Irish queen's right to the ancestral Ó Máille lands.

ALTERNATIVE ENQUIRY: WHAT CAN WE LEARN FROM GRACE O'MALLEY ABOUT SIXTEENTH-CENTURY IRELAND? (CHANGE AND CONTINUITY)

This enquiry sees pupils gathering evidence about O'Malley's life from a series of clues, working towards the curation of a Trip Advisor-style tour on locations linked to O'Malley's life. First, pupils record information about different aspects or stages of O'Malley's life, using a grid with headings including *Youth and early life*, *Marriage to Ó Flaithbheartaigh*, *Marriage to Burke*, *O'Malley as clan leader*, *Meeting with Elizabeth* and *Later life*. It is important that the clues help pupils to situate O'Malley's story within the broader context of changing relations between Ireland and England in the sixteenth century. Pupils ought to understand, for example, that Henry VIII's decision to dissolve the monasteries in Ireland and subdue the Irish chieftains in the 1542 Crown of Ireland Act would have created resentment towards the English Crown amongst the Ó Máille leaders. The increasing encroachment of the English was exemplified by the founding of plantations under Mary I and Elizabeth I, with these moves causing conflict between Irish leaders and English colonists.

Ultimately, pupils can be given map templates with some of the key sites of O'Malley's life plotted on, and they can be challenged to create tours that might be undertaken by historians and travellers wishing to develop their knowledge of Grace O'Malley and her significance in the sixteenth century. These sites might include Belclare Castle, the place of O'Malley's birth and one of the strongholds of the Ó Máille clan; Clare Island, the seat of O'Malley's own power as she established herself as head of the clan; Blacksod Bay, the site of O'Malley's vengeful attack on her lover's murderers; and Greenwich Palace, where O'Malley's famous meeting with Queen Elizabeth took place in 1593. Pupils can write brief overviews of each site for their tourists, explaining why the site was significant and how it links in with the broader story of relations between Ireland and England during the period.

O'Malley's story helps to exemplify some of the manifestations of power, with the clash between two powerful women (O'Malley and Elizabeth) serving to disrupt misconceptions about male supremacy during the early modern period. O'Malley's story also has wider importance as an episode within the turbulent history of relations between Ireland and England. It helps pupils to grasp some of the longer-term causes of recent conflicts, adding nuance to pupils' understanding of the English as colonisers in the sixteenth century and beyond.

KEY POINTS

- Grace O'Malley rose to become head of the Ó Máille clan in western Ireland.

- In 1593, O'Malley met with Elizabeth I at Greenwich Palace to petition for her right to the ancestral Ó Máille lands to be respected.

- O'Malley's request was granted, and the meeting stands as a landmark moment in the history of English relations with Ireland.

- O'Malley's story can be used to exemplify some of the manifestations of female power in the early modern period.

ELIZABETH ALKIN/ PARLIAMENT JOAN

- **Suggested enquiry:** How did spies like Elizabeth Alkin change the course of the English Civil War? (Significance)

- **Alternative enquiry:** How did the English Civil War change the lives of ordinary people in England? (Consequence/Change and continuity)

Whilst it is probably ill advised to share this with our pupils, there are inevitably some topics and time periods that we as teachers find less engaging. For me, the English Civil War is one of these topics. I did not enjoy learning about it when I was at school myself, and I found little reason to reassess my view when I first began teaching it – until I came across the story of the Civil War-era nurse, writer and spy Elizabeth Alkin (who sometimes went by the nickname Parliament Joan). A focus on the experiences and impact of Alkin sheds new light on the Civil War, allowing us to teach the tumultuous events of the 1640s from the perspective of women (who are sidelined from traditional accounts of the period) and, furthermore, to complicate notions of the Civil War as an exclusively political event.[12]

Born around the turn of the seventeenth century, Alkin first appeared in the historical record in 1645 when she was paid £2 (equivalent to at least £200 today) by the Committee for the Advance of Money, an organisation established by the Parliamentary forces during the Civil War. She was paid this amount for 'severall [sic] discoveries'; soon after, she received a further 40 shillings on account of her having 'discovered Geo. Mynne's wire'.[13] George Mynnes was an iron merchant who was supplying metal (a raw material to be put to use in warfare) to the royalist forces; it seems that Alkin was responsible for exposing his disloyal activities. Alkin was also involved in uncovering and divulging the authors of royalist publications

---

12 For more about the role of women during the Civil War, see The National Archives, 'Women and the English Civil Wars' (n.d.). Available at: https://www.nationalarchives.gov.uk/education/resources/women-english-civil-wars/.

13 J. J. Keevil, 'Elizabeth Alkin "Alias" Parliament Joan', *Bulletin of the History of Medicine* 31(1) (1957): 17–28 at 19.

to Parliamentarian forces. Later, she wrote her own pamphlets in support of the Parliamentarians.[14] It is clear that Alkin and other women of the time carried out their work in the face of significant prejudice. Contemporary publications emphasised the untrustworthy nature of women, and there was particular concern after the establishment of Cromwell's Commonwealth that the obscuring of class distinction had caused women to fall to the level of the uncultivated and promiscuous, with no privilege of rank or class to protect them. Still, Alkin continued to serve on behalf of the Parliamentarian/Commonwealth forces late in life; when Cromwell's Commonwealth forces went to war against the Dutch in the First Anglo-Dutch War of 1652–1654, Alkin helped to set up a network of hospitals to treat both English and Dutch casualties.

HOW DID SPIES LIKE ELIZABETH ALKIN CHANGE THE COURSE OF THE ENGLISH CIVIL WAR? (SIGNIFICANCE)

It is always instructive to begin an enquiry focused on spies with an exploration of pupils' preconceived ideas (and, in many cases, misconceptions). In a later enquiry on Cold War-era spy Oleg Gordievsky (see page 134), I describe pupils' surprise when they learn that children's author Roald Dahl was a spy, and pupils are equally baffled to learn that Elizabeth Alkin – a wife, nurse and, perhaps most importantly, a woman – can indeed be counted amongst the ranks of history's most guileful and imaginative spies.

Next, pupils can complete a card sort in their pairs, organising information about Alkin's life into chronological order. This can be done using a grid if cutting out the cards seems too time-consuming a task, although I find that the physical arrangement of the cards on the desk can be more conducive to discussion – and, of course, it allows for pupils to change their minds in a way that writing numbers or colouring in sections of a grid does not.

Once pupils have developed their understanding of the key events in Alkin's life, a further set of cards can be distributed; ensuring that these cards are printed on

---

14 For more about Civil War-era pamphleteering, see Marcus Nevitt, *Women and the Pamphlet Culture of Revolutionary England, 1640–1660* (London: Taylor & Francis, 2017).

a different colour paper is a simple way of ensuring that the activity remains manageable. These cards contain information about the context of the Civil War and pupils are tasked with organising the information into chronological order, just above their Alkin cards. At this point, pupils are asked to consider what might have happened if, for example, Alkin had failed to uncover the work of George Mynnes – or if she had determined to lend her support to the Royalist cause instead. Productive discussion of counterfactual history is supported with reference to the cards, as pupils are able to physically remove one of the events of Alkin's life and then decide how this might have affected the course of events described elsewhere.

In teaching about conflicts like the English Civil War, the French Revolution and the First and Second World Wars, there is a tendency to isolate women's experiences from the main action, and to explore them largely through the lenses of social history – focusing, perhaps, on how women contributed to life on the home front. Of course, it is important for pupils to understand some of the ways in which conflict has historically impacted on ordinary life, but it does a disservice to women in the past if we leave pupils with the impression that women were confined to the home for the duration of the conflict in question. Elizabeth Alkin's story serves as a useful corrective to this notion, helping to place women back in the midst of the action – and underlining the impact that women often had on broader political, military and legal developments.

KEY POINTS

- Elizabeth Alkin – also known as Parliament Joan – worked as a spy for Parliamentary forces during the English Civil War.

- Alkin was well paid for her work, despite women being held in low esteem during the period of Cromwell's Commonwealth.

- Counterfactuals (or 'what ifs') can be explored through a card-sort activity. Pupils remove events from one aspect of the story and discuss ways in which this might have changed things.

- Alkin's story helps to underline the varied roles of women in conflicts like the Civil War.

TEMPERANCE LLOYD AND THE DEVON WITCHES

- **Suggested enquiry:** Why was Temperance Lloyd executed in 1682? (Causation)

- **Alternative enquiry:** How can historians find out about the seventeenth-century witch craze? (Evidential understanding)

In 1926, a back-street junction in the parish of Heavitree, Devon, was deemed the ideal location for a new petrol station. During the excavation of the site – needed so that new petrol tanks could be sunk into the ground – human remains were discovered at the apex of the junction. Within weeks, bones belonging to at least twenty individuals had been uncovered. Following further investigation, it was discovered that the site had once been home to a public gallows which had been in use from at least the beginning of the sixteenth century.[15]

Amongst those executed at these gallows were local rioters and rebels William Horsington, Richard Reeves and Edward Willis, all convicted in 1655, as well as Elizabeth Packard who was found guilty of poisoning her husband, and in 1750 met her end at Heavitree. However, the focus of this enquiry is Temperance Lloyd, who became one of the last people in England to be executed for witchcraft when she was hanged at Heavitree in 1682.

---

15 Exeter Memories, 'Gallows Cross – Heavitree' (27 July 2015). Available at: http://www.exetermemories. co.uk/em/_places/gallows-cross.php. This article provides an overview of the petrol station's excavation.

WHY WAS TEMPERANCE LLOYD
EXECUTED IN 1682? (CAUSATION)

Temperance Lloyd's story lends itself to an enquiry in which pupils are drip fed clues as they try to work out the crime Lloyd had committed and, later, the social, economic and political circumstances that prompted locals to call for the execution of this vulnerable, elderly woman. Early clues ought, then, to deepen pupils' awareness of the historical context – and, perhaps, to provide a few red herrings in order to pique pupils' interest regarding what really happened to Lloyd. Pupils might learn, for example, that Heavitree and its surrounds had been an important trading post in the sixteenth and seventeenth centuries, as tobacco from the new English colony of Virginia was brought to the area before being exported to other places in Europe; this trade made some locals (including the explorer Sir Richard Grenville) very rich, although there was increasing resentment caused by the high taxes imposed on luxury goods like tobacco. This information might lend pupils the (false) impression that the crime of smuggling featured in Lloyd's story; if this enquiry was delivered as part of a GCSE Crime and Punishment unit, pupils' understanding of the social context would be developed, even as they contemplate and discard the information given to them in these misleading clues.

Subsequent clues might include extracts from the ballad that was written about Lloyd and two other accused women in 1682 ('But now it most apparent does appear, / That they will now for such their deeds pay dear: / For Satan, having lull'd their Souls asleep, / Refused Company with them to keep'),[16] comments made by Lloyd herself in the moments before her execution ('Jesus Christ speed me well; Lord forgive all my sins; Lord Jesus Christ be merciful to my poor soul') and extracts from the evidence provided at Lloyd's trial ('Eastchurch said that yesterday, the second of July, he did hear Temperance Lloyd say and confess that ... as she was returning home with a loaf of bread, she met with a man dressed all in black ... . The man tempted and persuaded her to visit Grace Thomas' house, and torment her').[17] Having studied these clues, pupils are likely to recognise that

---

16 The ballad, titled 'Witchcraft Discovered and Punished', is available at: https://quod.lib.umich.edu/e/eebo/B06662.0001.001/1:1?rgn=div1;view=fulltext.

17 A full account of the trial, including the evidence produced, can be found in Paul Karkeek, *Devonshire Witches* [eBook] (Urbana, IL: Project Gutenberg, 2020 [1874]). Available at: https://www.gutenberg.org/files/62273/62273.txt. For more information, see Ian Mortimer, *The Time Traveller's Guide to Restoration Britain* (London: Penguin, 2017) and Frank J. Gent, *The Trial of the Bideford Witches* (Bideford: Lazarus Press, 1982). These books offer overviews of this particular witch trial.

Lloyd's supposed crime was witchcraft, and that she was presumed to have brought about the death of a local woman following consultation with the Devil.

In the next stage of the enquiry, pupils could examine a second set of clues; this activity shifts the focus towards an investigation of the reasons for the witchcraft accusations levelled at Lloyd, as pupils are challenged to articulate the contextual factors that encouraged ordinary people to accuse their neighbours of this crime. Here, pupils might study information relating to the local population. The region suffered from a series of plague and smallpox epidemics in the 1600s, although an influx of refugees from France (persecuted for their religion) ensured that the population continued to grow. There is evidence, too, that Heavitree and its surrounds were home to a large number of Nonconformists; during the reign of Charles II (1630–1685), Catholics were punished harshly, especially following the failed (fictitious) Popish Plot of 1679. Pupils might consider the dislocating impact that these changing demographics might have exerted, and the extent to which these contextual factors help to explain the accusations levelled at Lloyd and other vulnerable women.

Finally, pupils might be challenged to update the existing plaque that commemorates the execution of Temperance Lloyd and three other local women at Heavitree. Though comprehensive in its recounting of the event ('The Devon Witches … The last people in England to be executed for witchcraft tried here & hanged at Heavitree'),[18] the plaque nevertheless fails to sufficiently account for the social, economic and political factors that combined to make fairly absurd accusations of sorcery and magical art seem credible.

Temperance Lloyd's story represents an opportunity to humanise the study of witchcraft in the seventeenth century, as pupils begin to understand the impact that wider political developments and social uncertainties wrought upon local communities – and, ultimately, the manner in which women like Lloyd were scapegoated for these difficulties.[19]

KEY POINTS

- Temperance Lloyd was one of the last women in England to be executed for the crime of witchcraft.

---

18 For more about the plaque, see: https://exetercivicsociety.org.uk/plaques/devon-witches/.
19 For more about the wider witch trials, see Brian P. Levack, *The Witch-Hunt in Early Modern Europe* (London: Routledge, 2013).

- Lloyd and two other women were executed in 1682. They were found guilty of consulting with the Devil.

- Using a drip-feed approach helps pupils develop a wider understanding of the social and economic factors that contributed to a surge in witchcraft accusations during the period.

THE ORIGINAL OLIVER TWIST: ROBERT BLINCOE

- **Suggested enquiry:** What was it like to be a worker during the Industrial Revolution? (Similarity and difference)
- **Alternative enquiry:** How can we use Robert Blincoe's autobiography to find out about child labour during the Victorian period? (Evidential understanding)

One of my favourite things about Victorian-era books, pamphlets and tracts is that it is possible to gain a relatively good idea of the message to be conveyed in the text by the title – which usually runs to at least four or five lines, with the most important or attention-grabbing phrases benefitting from large or emboldened print. In the case of Robert Blincoe's autobiography (first published in 1832), the title all but gives the entire book away: *A Memoir of Robert Blincoe, an Orphan Boy; sent from the workhouse of St Pancras, London, at seven years of age, to endure the Horrors of a Cotton-Mill, through his infancy and youth, with a minute detail of his sufferings, being The First Memoir of the Kind Published.* The book's preface under-lines the polemic nature of the work, with the author comparing the machinations of the industrial-era factory to the 'Negro slave-trade' in its exploitation of workers (particularly children). Finally, the preface attacks Member of Parliament William Wilberforce who, the author writes, might have done a good deal to advocate for the rights of enslaved men and women abroad, but had done little to improve the lot of the 'white infant-slaves' who spun the slave-grown cotton into products fit for an eager yet uncaring British public.[20]

The book's author, Robert Blincoe, was born in 1792, and appears to have been orphaned as a baby or toddler: by the age of four he was registered at the St. Pancras workhouse in London. Blincoe was employed for a short time as a chimney sweep, before being sold to work at a cotton mill near Nottingham. According to

---

20 Robert Blincoe, *A Memoir of Robert Blincoe* (Manchester: J. Doherty, 1832), p. iii.

his autobiography, Blincoe had at first been 'intoxicated with joy' at the thought of his new employment. The workhouse children had been informed that their 'apprenticeship' at the cotton mill would see them 'transformed' into ladies and gentlemen, and 'that they would be fed on roast beef and plum-pudding ... and have silver watches, and plenty of cash in their pockets.'[21] Such expectations were violently quashed when the true nature of the workers' exploitation was revealed: the children worked fourteen hours a day, six days a week, were given only porridge and black bread to eat and crammed into unsanitary dormitories at night. Blincoe worked as a mule scavenger, collecting loose cotton threads from below the spinning machines – although as the machines could not be turned off, the job was extremely dangerous. Blincoe recalled one girl of around 10 being drawn into the machine when her apron became caught in the frame: she was 'whirled round and round with the shaft', and her bones were snapped and crushed by its deadly machinations.[22] According to his autobiography, Blincoe attempted suicide several times. Finally, he completed his *apprenticeship* and was later able to establish his own cotton-spinning business. Some historians believe that Charles Dickens based the character of Oliver Twist on the childhood experiences of Blincoe.

WHAT WAS IT LIKE TO BE A WORKER DURING THE INDUSTRIAL REVOLUTION? (SIMILARITY AND DIFFERENCE)

Robert Blincoe's story sits best within a scheme of work according to which the basics of the Industrial Revolution have already been established, and pupils have an understanding of the fundamental interrelationships between the slave trade and the stimulation of British industrial growth. If this has already been explored, pupils will be able to make sense of the huge investment (financial as well as physical) that underpinned the explosion of British factory production; it is also easier to contextualise Blincoe's rather problematic comparison between enslaved men and women and child labourers. Working towards being able to respond to the enquiry question, pupils can study evidence from a range of sources including Blincoe's autobiography, as well as evidence relating to biscuit factory workers

---

21 Blincoe, *A Memoir*, pp. 13–14.
22 Blincoe, *A Memoir*, p. 27.

(perhaps at Huntley and Palmers, a company employed in biscuit making since 1822), domestic servants and chimney sweeps.[23] A Key Stage 2 enquiry I planned saw pupils organise this information into a diagram identifying evidence relating to two categories; *Everyday life* and *Dangers*. At Key Stage 3, pupils might use a Venn diagram focusing instead on the ways in which capitalist factory owners, the people of England and child workers themselves benefitted from the exploitation of child labour. In either case, pupils can be encouraged to respond in full to the enquiry question, outlining ways in which workers' experiences were (for example) positive, negative, improving or worsening during the nineteenth century.

Blincoe was, of course, a success story – although many of the other child labourers of Victorian Britain were not. We will never know the details of their lives, precisely because they did not have the opportunity to record their experiences and observations for posterity. It is important, therefore, that we take the chance wherever we can to give voice to ordinary people from the past and to examine the ways in which their lives were shaped by those in more powerful positions than their own.

KEY POINTS

● Robert Blincoe worked as a mule scavenger at a Nottingham-based cotton mill.

● Blincoe later described his experiences in his autobiography, and some historians think that Charles Dickens based the character of Oliver Twist on Blincoe.

● In the enquiry, pupils compare Blincoe's experiences with those of other child workers, including workers at a biscuit factory, domestic servants and chimney sweeps.

● Blincoe's story helps give voice to ordinary workers of the industrial era.

---

23 See T. A. B. Corley, *Quaker Enterprise in Biscuits: Huntley and Palmers of Reading, 1822–1972* (London: Hutchinson, 1972); William Lanceley, *From Hall-Boy to House-Steward* (London: Edward Arnold & Co., 1925); David Porter, *Consideration on the Present State of Chimney Sweepers* (London: T. Burton, 1792). These books can be used to find extracts relating to the experiences of biscuit-factory workers, domestic servants and chimney sweeps. See also Jane Humphries, *Childhood and Child Labour in the British Industrial Revolution* (Cambridge: Cambridge University Press, 2010). This book gives a useful overview of different types of child workers and their experiences during the period.

JOSEPHINE BUTLER AND 'THE DOUBLE STANDARD OF MORALITY'

> ● **Suggested enquiry:** What impact did Josephine Butler have on the lives of working-class Victorian women? (Significance/Consequence)
>
> ● **Alternative enquiry:** How did women's lives change in the nineteenth century? (Change and continuity)

In 1886, feminist and social reformer Josephine Butler wrote an article entitled 'The Double Standard of Morality'. In the article, she attacked the tendency according to which male 'immorality' was condoned and even tacitly encouraged, whilst women were condemned for any behaviour judged to have transgressed established moral and sexual norms. She wrote, 'here we are at once brought into contact with the false and misleading idea that the essence of right and wrong is in some way dependent on sex. We never hear it carelessly or complacently asserted of a young woman that "she is only sowing her wild oats."' Women who fell foul of accusations of 'impurity' were 'hurled to despair', whilst the rest of 'womanhood' was 'kept strictly and almost forcibly guarded in domestic purity'; there was no freedom at either end of the spectrum. Butler declared it her mission to 'Christianise public opinion' until it was widely understood that the 'essence' of morality was not dependent upon sex – and until the same demands for purity and chastity were made of both men and women.[24]

Butler was born in 1828 into a deeply religious, politically progressive family. She married at the age of 24 and, upon moving to Oxford with her new husband, became concerned about the plight of several vulnerable women in the city. Hearing about a woman who had been seduced and then abandoned by a university don – and who had, in desperation, murdered her baby – Butler arranged for

---

24 Josephine Butler, 'The Double Standard of Morality', *W. B. Stead Resource Site*. First published in *The Philanthropist* (October 1886). Available at: https://www.attackingthedevil.co.uk/related/morality.php.

the woman to serve part of her prison sentence in the Butlers' own home. Butler became a passionate advocate of women's rights, and in 1869 she was appointed secretary of the Ladies' National Association for the Repeal of the Contagious Diseases Acts. These Acts – introduced in a supposed attempt to regulate prostitution – allowed the authorities to detain all women working as prostitutes in port towns in order that they undergo intrusive medical examinations. Those who refused could be imprisoned. Those who submitted to the examination were placed on a register, their inclusion on which effectively barred them from all opportunities for *respectable* future employment. The male *clients* of these prostitutes were not required to undergo any form of examination. Butler and the Ladies' National Association finally succeeded in bringing about the Acts' repeal in 1886. Butler continued to advocate for social causes for the rest of her life, including Irish Home Rule, the exposure of police corruption, and women's suffrage. She even lobbied for the repeal of laws in India which – like those that had been in place in Britain – compelled prostitutes to undergo intrusive medical examination.[25]

WHAT IMPACT DID JOSEPHINE BUTLER HAVE ON THE LIVES OF WORKING-CLASS VICTORIAN WOMEN? (SIGNIFICANCE/CONSEQUENCE)

Butler is one of my favourite Victorians. Whilst she certainly epitomises the do-good spirit of the age, she was also clearly motivated by a genuine passion for women's rights and she was not afraid to challenge patriarchal society for the double standards that she identified. Her writings would no doubt have been highly controversial should policymakers have heeded the messages she imparted; Butler was unrelenting in her belief that religion had been misused and misappropriated by those wishing to excuse men of behaviours that would have been 'fiercely condemned' in women.[26] This enquiry ought to, therefore, make room for a nuanced and contextualised examination of Butler and her work, allowing pupils

---

25 See Helen Mathers, *Patron Saint of Prostitutes: Josephine Butler and a Victorian Scandal* (Cheltenham: The History Press, 2014). This book provides an overview of Butler's campaigns.
26 Butler, 'The Double Standard of Morality'.

to appreciate the extent to which Butler challenged the norms and values under-pinning Victorian society.

We need to be careful in employing combative analogies in the teaching and learning activities that we use, not least because they promote the problematic view that there were only two sides in historic conflicts. However, in the case of Butler's crusade against mid-Victorian sexual inequality, the analogy is appropri-ate – and so I structure this enquiry around the idea of a tug of war. Pupils deepen their knowledge of Butler and the work she carried out by reading an overview of the campaigns in which she participated. Then they are challenged to label figures from a cartoon tug-of-war diagram; on one side are figures representing the chal-lenges or inequalities that Butler identified, and on the other are figures representing the actions or initiatives undertaken by Butler to fight against these issues.

Ultimately, it is up to pupils to determine who won and they reach their conclu-sions based on an evaluation of the evidence relating to Butler's impact and legacy. The tributes made to Butler by later suffrage campaigners (including Millicent Fawcett, who hailed Butler as 'the most distinguished Englishwoman of the nineteenth century'[27]) deserve to be highlighted here, to help pupils recognise the extent to which Butler laid the foundations for the militant feminist move-ments of the twentieth and twenty-first centuries.

KEY POINTS

- Josephine Butler was a social reformer who identified a double standard in attitudes towards male and female sexuality.

- Butler successfully campaigned for the repeal of the Contagious Diseases Acts, as well as lending her support to a number of other social causes.

- It is important that pupils understand the groundwork laid by women like Butler, and the debt that twentieth-century suffragists owed to Butler's campaigns.

---

27 Roxanne Eberle, *Chastity and Transgression in Women's Writing, 1792–1897* (Basingstoke: Palgrave, 2002), p. 218.

ELIZA ARMSTRONG AND 'THE MAIDEN TRIBUTE OF MODERN BABYLON'

- **Suggested enquiry:** What does the case of Eliza Armstrong tell us about life in Victorian Britain? (Significance)
- **Alternative enquiry:** How successful were the Social Purity movements of the nineteenth century? (Consequence/Change and continuity)

On 4 July 1885, the *Pall Mall Gazette* issued a 'frank warning' to its middle-class Victorian readers: 'All those who are squeamish, and all those who are prudish, and all those who would prefer to live in a fool's paradise of imaginary innocence and purity, selfishly oblivious to the horrible realities which torment those whose lives are passed in the London inferno, will do well not to read the *Pall Mall Gazette* on Monday and the three following days.'[28] The 'warning' had the intended effect, and when the first editorial – with one subtitle which read 'The Violation of Virgins' – was published two days later, the appetite of the public had been whetted and conservative England was ready to be whipped into a frenzy by the exposé that followed. W. T. Stead (the newspaper's editor, as well as the author of the series of articles known as 'The Maiden Tribute of Modern Babylon') explained that his 'careful and painstaking inquiry' had elicited evidence of a child prostitution epidemic in London and beyond. Some children, Stead explained, 'are simply snared, trapped and outraged either when under the influence of drugs or after a prolonged struggle in a locked room', whilst others 'are regularly procured … or enticed under various promises into the fatal chamber from which they are never allowed to emerge.' Stead contended that there were five types of crime in which the authorities were honour-bound to intervene; these included the 'sale and

---

28 W. T. Stead, 'Notice to our Readers: A Frank Warning', *W. B. Stead Resource Site*. First published in *The Pall Mall Gazette* (4 July 1885). Available at: https://www.attackingthedevil.co.uk/pmg/tribute/notice.php.

purchase and violation of children', the 'entrapping and ruin of women' and 'the international slave trade in girls'.[29]

Stead's findings were disquieting, but it was the methods by which he had acquired his evidence that attracted the most attention. In relating the story of 'A Child of Thirteen bought for £5', Stead obscured the fact that it had been he himself who had initially purchased the 'human chattel' in question. Changing the girl's name from Eliza to Lily, Stead described the process by which Lily was procured for the sum of £5 (£3 'paid down' and the remaining £2 to be paid once her virginity had been 'certified'). Lily was taken from her mother – who was apparently so drunk that she hardly recognised her daughter – and a certificate of virginity was gained following an 'inspection' carried out by a midwife; Lily was then taken to a 'house of ill fame' and pacified with the help of some chloroform. Most shockingly, Stead then related that 'the purchaser entered the bedroom. He closed and locked the door. There was a brief silence. And then there rose a wild and piteous cry ... a helpless, startled scream like the bleat of a frightened lamb. And the child's voice was heard crying, in accents of terror, "There's a man in the room! Take me home; oh, take me home!" And then all once more was still.'[30]

Stead's articles caused uproar in Britain and beyond. Politicians called for the immediate cessation of the editorials' publication and social reformers organised protest meetings, taking advantage of the widespread panic engendered amongst the public to campaign for a change in the law. The articles also had unintended consequences; when it was discovered that Stead himself had been the original purchaser of Lily, he – along with others involved in the investigation – was charged with the assault and abduction of Eliza Armstrong. Stead was found guilty and sentenced to three months' imprisonment. He continued to edit the *Pall Mall Gazette* during his time in prison, enjoying an increased readership. The prosecutor in Stead's case initiated a public subscription (or fundraising event) for Eliza Armstrong, and the money raised paid for her to attend a training home for girls wishing to become servants; she went on to marry twice and have ten children. Eliza and Stead remained on friendly terms until Stead was killed during the sinking of the *Titanic* in 1912.

---

29 W. T. Stead, 'The Maiden Tribute of Modern Babylon I: The Report of our Secret Commission', *W. B. Stead Resource Site*. First published in *The Pall Mall Gazette* (6 July 1885). Available at: https://www. attackingthedevil.co.uk/pmg/tribute/mt1.php.
30 Stead, 'The Maiden Tribute of Modern Babylon I'.

WHAT DOES THE CASE OF ELIZA ARMSTRONG TELL US ABOUT LIFE IN VICTORIAN BRITAIN? (SIGNIFICANCE)

The story of Eliza Armstrong can be situated within a study of late-Victorian Britain, to exemplify some of the themes that might otherwise have been highlighted in an enquiry on Jack the Ripper. Of course, the Ripper and his crimes make for highly engaging lesson content, but it is so easy to implicitly affirm the very stereotypes that we are hoping to challenge – especially when the Ripper's supposed foreign-ness (and his presumed links to the poverty-stricken Russian Jewry) are explored. By instead using the Armstrong case study to learn about poverty, exploitation, vice and the nature of life in an industrial city, we can offer pupils a more complex and less problematic picture of this period in the past.

In the enquiry, pupils can extract evidence from Stead's articles, as well as infor-mation about Stead and his court case. They develop an understanding of the moral panics that gripped polite Victorian society – and the strange, evangelising impulses that drove London's well-to-do to go *slumming* (essentially, integrating themselves into the East End slums in a bid to experience the squalid conditions for themselves).[31] In a creative final activity, pupils are inspired by Jack London's famous book *The People of the Abyss* (1903) to compose their own travelogues, describing what they would have expected to find on a journey through London in the late nineteenth century.[32]

KEY POINTS

- 'The Maiden Tribute of Modern Babylon' was a series of articles written by W. T. Stead in 1885, exposing the high incidence of child prostitution in London and beyond.

- Eliza Armstrong was the subject of Stead's exposé.

- Armstrong was the victim of a trafficking incident that Stead himself instigated (in the name of investigative journalism).

---

31 Seth Koven, *Slumming: Sexual and Social Politics in Victorian London* (Princeton, NJ: Princeton University Press, 2006). In this book, Koven examines the fashion for slumming.
32 Jack London, *The People of the Abyss* [eBook] (Urbana, IL: Project Gutenberg, 1999). Available at: https://www.gutenberg.org/files/1688/1688-h/1688-h.htm.

- Armstrong's story allows pupils to explore life in a late-Victorian industrial city; it is perhaps a more appropriate vehicle for studying this theme than, for example, the story of Jack the Ripper.

Aruna Asaf Ali, see page 110.

Chapter 4
POWER AND POLITICS (WIDER WORLD)

INTRODUCTION

In seeking to reflect the diverse and contingent nature of power and politics in a wider-world context, our biggest enemy is tokenism. There are so many topics that present themselves as opportunities for exploring the manifestations of power. The *History Programmes of Study: Key Stage 3* document suggests Mughal India, China's Qing dynasty, the changing Russian empires and USA in the twentieth century.[1] Significant work has also been done by historians in recommending the African kingdoms of Asante, Kongo, Songhay and Benin as fruitful sites for the exploration of monarchy, government and other structures of power.[2] However, it is important that we resist the urge to offer too sweeping a study of these governments and rulers, as doing so would risk skimming the surface – and thereby making flawed claims and generalisations about the ways in which power was both exercised and challenged in very different times, places and contexts.

The case studies in this section – situated in early modern Benin, imperial Russia, early twentieth-century America, Nazi Germany and twentieth-century India, respectively – are intended to complement and complicate existing schemes of work on the nature of power in these contexts. The individuals whose experiences are featured can offer new insight into the ways in which authority and influence was exercised in the past, as well as the ways *ordinary* people challenged and appropriated power in unexpected and significant ways. Their stories are not intended to be inspiring in any straightforward way, but they do serve to illustrate the complicated and contested nature of political, legal, social and cultural authority – and to demonstrate the extent to which power might sometimes be wielded by those we consider the least capable of doing so.

---

1   Department for Education, *History Programmes of Study: Key Stage 3*.
2   For example, see Toby Green, *History A: African Kingdoms: A Guide to the Kingdoms of Songhay, Kongo, Benin, Oyo and Dahomey c.1400–c.1800* [eBook] (OCR, 2015). Available at: https://www.ocr.org.uk/Images/208299-african-kingdoms-ebook-.pdf.

IDIA, THE QUEEN MOTHER OF BENIN

- **Suggested enquiry:** How did Queen Idia help to bring about the golden age of Benin? (Causation)
- **Alternative enquiry:** Did the Obas of Benin really rule through violence and superstition? (Interpretations)

The kingdom of Benin (situated in modern-day Nigeria) was one of the most powerful African kingdoms of the early modern period. Established in the eleventh century when – according to oral histories – village chiefs requested a divine ruler to restore order in the region, Benin enjoyed what historians have since termed a golden age in the fifteenth and sixteenth centuries. The development of new trade links helping to confirm the kingdom's status and wealth, and when Portuguese explorers first arrived in the 1480s, the kingdom was at the height of its power.

Benin was ruled by Obas, who oversaw law and order within the kingdom as well as leading military expeditions with the aim of consolidating more land and extending the empire. Although the Obas were male, it is clear that women played an essential role in government. The wife of the serving Oba was expected to raise the prince who would eventually succeed his father, and once her son was crowned she became known as the Iyoba (a title similar in some ways to 'Queen Mother'). The Iyoba was considered a chief of relatively high rank and in times of war she was able to command her own military regiment. If the Iyoba died during the reign of her son, she became the patron goddess of the Oba: a significant honour.[3]

---

3   See Toby Green, *History A: African Kingdoms.* This eBook provides a useful overview of life in some of the African kingdoms that were powerful during the early modern period, including the kingdom of Benin.

HOW DID QUEEN IDIA HELP TO BRING ABOUT THE GOLDEN AGE OF BENIN? (CAUSATION)

One of the most well-known Iyobas of Benin was Queen Idia. In the late fifteenth century, Benin was ruled by Idia's husband Ozolua, who helped to expand the empire through a number of military successes (as well as establishing important trade links with the Portuguese). However, when Ozolua died there was a succession crisis as both of Ozolua's sons – Esigie and Arualan – claimed the title of Oba for themselves. Civil war ensued, and the conflict threatened to undermine Benin's status and power. It was at this point that Idia made a number of crucial interventions on the part of one of her sons, Esigie. Oral traditions claim that she raised an army on his behalf, and she directed her political counsel (as well as medicinal knowledge and mystical powers) towards the aim of confirming Esigie's status as Oba. Esigie conferred significant privileges and power on his mother during the course of his reign (perhaps creating the title 'Iyoba' in recognition of her importance), and the large number of artistic depictions of Idia that were looted from Benin during the British Benin Expedition of 1897 indicate the esteem in which she was held at Oba Esigie's court. This causation enquiry can be used to facilitate an exploration of the successes of the kingdom of Benin, and to underline the important role played by women in this early modern kingdom. Indeed, it would be productive to consider some of the similarities and differences between the power and status of women in early modern Africa and Europe, and to note some of the ways in which the kingdom of Benin was characterised by a more progressive attitude towards women.

ALTERNATIVE ENQUIRY: DID THE OBAS OF BENIN REALLY RULE THROUGH VIOLENCE AND SUPERSTITION? (INTERPRETATIONS)

Alternatively, this interpretation-focused enquiry encourages pupils to dismantle some of the false dichotomies that have been created between Africa and the West – particularly, in this case, with regard to the nature of violence, superstition and mysticism in the African kingdoms. Pupils might first be given an extract from the book *The City of Blood* by Reginald H. Bacon, Commander of the British expedition to Benin in 1897. Bacon described the 'crucifixions, human sacrifices, and every horror the eye could get accustomed to', noting that 'blood was everywhere; smeared over bronzes, ivory, and even the walls.'[4] Bacon suggested that the sights and smells were such that 'no white man's internal economy could stand.'[5] Pupils might then be asked to explore how much of Bacon's observations can be supported with evidence, as they seek to respond to the enquiry question. To do this, pupils can plot information onto a radar graph, deciding the extent to which the evidence suggests first that the Obas ruled through violence and superstition or reason and representation and, second, whether the Obas ruled effectively or ineffectively. Radar graphs work well for this activity as they allow pupils to make two judgements simultaneously.

Once pupils have determined that, on the whole, the Obas appear to have ruled through reason and representation rather than violence and superstition, the enquiry can be extended by asking pupils to examine two other accounts that proved instrumental in shaping misconceptions about the Kingdom of Benin. One of these accounts is John Adams' *Remarks on the Country Extending from Cape Palmas to the River Congo* (1823); the other is Henry Ling Roth's *Great Benin: Its Customs, Art and Horrors* (1903).[6] Once pupils understand that the former of these accounts was written during the period of British colonial expansion and the latter soon after the British had successfully colonised the Kingdom of Benin, they should be able to comment on some of the reasons why these accounts might offer a somewhat flawed impression of life under the Obas of Benin.

Lending greater nuance to pupils' understanding of Africa in the early modern period is an essential task of history teachers; we must undermine notions of African incivility and backwardness. An enquiry focused on the power of the Obas helps to emphasise the African kingdoms' autonomy and sophistication in the fifteenth and sixteenth centuries – it also serves, fundamentally, to divorce Africa and African history from traditional associations with the slave trade, foregrounding the richness of precolonial African history before the incursion of the Europeans.

---

4   Reginald. H. Bacon, *The City of Blood* (London: Arnold, 1897), p. 84.
5   Bacon, *The City*, p. 96.
6   John Adams, *Remarks on the Country Extending from Cape Palmas to the River Congo* (London: G and W. B. Whittaker, 1823); H. Ling Roth, *Great Benin: Its Customs, Art and Horrors* (Halifax: F. King, 1903).

KEY POINTS

- Queen Idia was the mother of Esigie, Oba of Benin from 1504 to 1550. She helped him claim the throne and went on to play an important role in his consolidation of power.

- The title 'Iyoba' recognised the status conferred to the Obas' mothers during Benin's golden age.

- Misconceptions about the nature of life in Benin can be challenged through an interpretations enquiry.

- It is important that we make room within our curricula for the study of Africa before the Europeans' arrival.

SHE 'DARES ARRAIGN IMPERIAL CRIME': SOPHIA PEROVSKAYA

- **Suggested enquiry:** Why was Sophia Perovskaya executed in 1881? (Causation)

- **Alternative enquiry:** How significant were female revolutionaries in nineteenth-century Russia? (Significance/Change and continuity)

The Russian Revolution is an exciting topic of study, and the characters of Lenin, Stalin and Trotsky – as well as lesser-known individuals like Bukharin, Tukhachevsky and Koltsov – make good subjects for enquiries at Key Stages 3, 4 and 5. However, pupils would be forgiven for coming away from this topic believing that the only roles available for women in tsarist and communist Russia were as wives, mothers or low-paid workers. It is important to seek out stories of real women who experienced these tumultuous times, some of whom exerted a significant impact on events in pre- and post-revolutionary Russia.

Born in 1853, Sophia Perovskaya lived through the heady days of reform and emancipation instituted by the 'Tsar Liberator' Alexander II; peasants were released from their traditional servitude, local government was given new freedoms, education opportunities were broadened and censorship was radically reduced. However, during Perovskaya's teenage years she would have witnessed the effects of Alexander's disastrous counter-reforms, as the aging tsar – increasingly alienated from the radical elements of his own family – reversed many of his progressive policies. Suddenly, extremist organisations and underground printing presses were springing up across Russia's newly industrialising cities, with universities offering a breeding ground for a new generation of revolutionaries baying for Alexander's blood.

WHY WAS SOPHIA PEROVSKAYA EXECUTED IN 1881? (CAUSATION)

At first glance, Sophia Perovskaya does not appear an obvious candidate for anarchism, born as she was into an aristocratic family that boasted connections with a former empress of Russia. It is partly for this reason that Perovskaya works as a case study for this topic; the mystery element of the enquiry can be maintained for some time, as pupils are confounded by Perovskaya's noble background and her familial links with the very centres of social privilege and authority. A drip-feed approach works well with this enquiry, with pupils encouraged to form and refine their hypotheses as they encounter new clues.

They will discover, for example, that Perovskaya spent her early years in Crimea; an area ravaged by fighting during the disastrous Crimean War. This might lead pupils to infer that Perovskaya's family – perhaps traitors to the partisan cause – found themselves on the losing side, and that the entire family was executed as punishment. Later, pupils read extracts from a poem written by Australian politician Henry Parkes about Perovskaya, in which Parkes warned that Perovskaya's 'beauteous lineaments of girlhood' served to obscure 'a force sublime / Which moulds to fearful use events / And dares arraign Imperial crime.'[7] Close reading of this source can be very productive; pupils might speculate about the 'force sublime' to which Parkes alluded, and consider what might have been deemed an 'Imperial crime'.

Ultimately, the clues lead pupils to recognise that Perovskaya was executed on grounds of her revolutionary activities. Perovskaya was radicalised during her time at university and joined the controversial literary society, Circle of Tchaikovsky. Perovskaya aligned herself with the terrorist organisation People's Will and worked to bring about the assassination of the tsar. Finally, the group was successful. Perovskaya was one of the revolutionaries stationed along the route of Alexander II's ill-fated drive through the streets of St Petersburg and was reportedly responsible for giving a signal to the bomb-throwing terrorists who targeted Alexander's carriage.

---

7 Henry Parkes, 'The Beauteous Terrorist', *The Libertarian Labyrinth*. Available at: https://www.libertarian-labyrinth.org/the-sex-question/sir-henry-parkes-the-beauteous-terrorist-sophie-perovskaya-1885/.

Causation is multifaceted, and it is important for pupils to recognise that they need to examine a range of factors or reasons. A causal-thinking quilt therefore helps pupils to prioritise information about the causes of Perovskaya's execution. Pupils need, too, to be able to explain how causes link together, and a causation map can be a useful way of helping pupils to visualise this as they draw lines between the different causes to show linkages between them. For example, pupils might recognise that a root cause of the execution was Perovskaya's youthful radicalisation, and that this radicalisation was, in turn, brought about by dissatisfaction with Alexander II's counter-reforming policies.

Perovskaya's femininity was not the most important thing about her, and it would be misleading to leave pupils with the impression that Perovskaya is only worthy of study because she was a woman. Nevertheless, it is interesting to consider the rather hagiographic approach that has been taken in memorialising this revolutionary figure, much of which seems to have been influenced considerably by Perovskaya's femininity. Indeed, even the prosecutor at Perovskaya's trial was affronted by the fact that Perovskaya – a woman – was such a devoted terrorist, noting 'That a woman should lead a conspiracy, that she should take on herself all the details of murder ... that a woman should have become the life and soul of this conspiracy – any normal feelings of mortality can have no understanding of such a role for women.'[8] Equally, it is no doubt in large part due to Perovskaya's gender that she was the subject of a famous 1967 Soviet film.[9] Therefore, pupils might be encouraged to reflect on issues of commemoration, considering the ways in which certain stories and individuals have captured the imagination of subsequent generations – and how history can be used and abused in the name of contemporary political agendas.

KEY POINTS

- Sophia Perovskaya was a revolutionary who helped to organise the assassination of Alexander II in 1881.

- Perovskaya was partly radicalised by the counter-reforming policies of Alexander II, as the tsar undermined many of his earlier reforms during the 1860s and 1870s.

---

8 John Simkin, 'Sophia Perovskaya', *Spartacus Educational* (September 1997). Available at: https://spartacus-educational.com/RUSperovskaya.htm.
9 *Sophia Perovskaya*, dir. by Lev Arnshtam [film] (Mosfilm, 1967).

- An enquiry focused on the reasons for Perovskaya's execution helps to underline the multifaceted nature of causation.

- Perovskaya's femininity partly accounts for her enduring renown, and this aspect of the story can be explored as part of the enquiry.

'TRESPASSERS, BEWARE!': LYDA CONLEY AND THE FIGHT FOR HURON CEMETERY

> ● **Suggested enquiry:** What was the impact of conflict between the US government and Indigenous Americans in the early twentieth century? (Consequence/Change and continuity)
>
> ● **Alternative enquiry:** Why did Lyda Conley come into conflict with the American government in 1910? (Causation)

In January 1910, lawyer Lyda Conley appeared before the Supreme Court – America's highest court of justice – to protest against the American government's contravention of a treaty that had been enacted in 1855. The treaty had been agreed between the Wyandotte people (an Indigenous American group that originated around the shores of Lake Ontario but had migrated to the lower-Midwestern region by the late nineteenth century) and the US government, and prevented the Wyandotte land from being sold. However, the US government was keen to sell the land for development. Conley's case was not in itself remarkable; disputes over land ownership between Indigenous Americans and the US government had been a feature of American political life throughout the nineteenth and early twentieth centuries, with most court rulings favouring the claims of the government representatives. However, Lyda Conley was herself remarkable, as she was the first Indigenous American woman to be admitted to the bar in Kansas – and, indeed, the first Indigenous American woman to argue a case before America's Supreme Court.

Lyda Conley was the daughter of Elizabeth Zane, a member of the Wyandotte people, and Andrew Conley, a migrant of English descent who met Lyda's mother when the Wyandotte were forced to move westwards due to the encroachment of the US government on their ancestral lands. The land over which Conley and the US government representatives fought was partly occupied by a Wyandotte burial ground called Huron Cemetery, where several of Conley's ancestors had been laid to rest. Ahead of her appearance before the Supreme Court, Conley built a hut close to the burial ground in which she and her sister could camp out, allowing them to protect the ground. They stood guard with muskets and erected 'Trespassers, Beware!' signs around the cemetery. Although the 1910 case was lost, Conley continued to campaign for the land's protection and, finally, in 1916 a bill was passed protecting the cemetery and determining that the land be made into a national park. Conley continued to protect the cemetery for the rest of her life, even after she was charged with arrest when she chased some people from the cemetery. Conley was murdered during a robbery in 1946 (the thief hit Conley with a brick and claimed the 20 cents that she carried in her bag). She was buried alongside the ancestors whose resting place she had dedicated her life to protecting.[10]

WHAT WAS THE IMPACT OF CONFLICT BETWEEN THE US GOVERNMENT AND INDIGENOUS AMERICANS IN THE EARLY TWENTIETH CENTURY? (CONSEQUENCE/ CHANGE AND CONTINUITY)

Lyda Conley's activities can help to complicate notions of the Indigenous Americans as the downtrodden victims of the US government and its increasingly rampant expansionist policies. This enquiry might focus, therefore, on the losses experienced by Indigenous Americans groups, but Conley's story serves as a reminder of the ways in which Indigenous American communities resisted incursions onto their land – and, indeed, the continued vibrancy of many Indigenous American cultural practices, beliefs and oral histories today.

In the enquiry, pupils can begin by categorising information on a thinking quilt, according to whether it describes *causes, events* or *consequences* of US government policy. Some of the *causes* might include stereotypical perceptions about Indigenous American backwardness, the US government's desire to expand westwards in order to claim large swathes of the continent, and US victory in the

---

10 For an overview of Conley's life, see Emma Rothberg, 'Lyda Conley', *National Women's History Museum* (2020). Available at: https://www.womenshistory.org/education-resources/biographies/lyda-conley.

Mexican–American War of 1846–1848 (resulting in American annexation of Texas and Oregon County – and the enclosure of Indigenous American territory by US states). *Events* describe the policies themselves, such as the establishment of the Bureau of Indian Affairs in 1824, the Indian Removal Act of 1830 and the Treaty of Fort Laramie in 1851. Finally, *consequences* include the forced removal of Indigenous American groups from their ancestral lands, the establishment of reservations, conflict between the US government and Indigenous American groups and, of course, the acts of resistance exemplified by the activities of Lyda Conley.

Pupils can analyse this information further; for example, they might be asked to judge the extent to which US government policy was characterised by an attempt to assimilate Indigenous Americans into American ways of life, or to help preserve and develop Indigenous American social and cultural practices. If taught as a GCSE enquiry, pupils might be required to apply their knowledge to a narrative-account response, in which they outline developments in US government policy. I like to end consequence-focused enquiries by providing pupils with a vocabulary bank and asking them to use this list of words and phrases to formulate a paragraph outlining the ways in which certain causes resulted in different outcomes and consequences. For example, pupils might decide that the notion of Manifest Destiny *encouraged* increasing numbers of travellers to migrate westward, that the inauguration of the Bureau of Indian Affairs *underpinned* the development of false dichotomies between Americans and Indigenous peoples, or that the building of reservations *sparked* conflict between US government and Indigenous American forces.

Ultimately, pupils need to understand that Indigenous Americans did not simply assent to US government encroachment onto their lands. There were important instances of resistance – many of which (like the activities of Lyda Conley) were entirely peaceable. Conley may have focused on conserving a single burial ground, but in her belligerent approach to the protection of her ancestral history and culture she represents a much broader impulse within the Indigenous American communities that lived in the American West in the nineteenth and twentieth centuries.

KEY POINTS

● Lyda Conley became the first Indigenous American woman to be admitted to the bar in Kansas.

- Conley protested against the US government's infringement on her ancestral lands.

- Through her sustained efforts, she successfully safeguarded Huron Cemetery against sale to developers.

- Conley's story helps to underline the ways in which Indigenous Americans resisted US government incursion on their lands and cultural practices.

GERTRUD SCHOLTZ-KLINK AND 'FASCINATING FASCISM'

- **Suggested enquiry:** What can we learn from Gertrud Scholtz-Klink about the experiences of women in Nazi Germany? (Similarity and difference)
- **Alternative enquiry:** Was Susan Sontag right about 'Fascinating Fascism'? (Interpretations)

In an influential essay called 'Fascinating Fascism' (published in 1974), American writer and activist Susan Sontag described the circumstances according to which ordinary people were compelled to follow – and in some cases dedicate themselves to – fascist regimes. Sontag's essay was intended as a warning of the possible resurgence of fascism in the 1970s, and she argued that such inducements as the 'drama of the leader and the chorus' attracted people to fascist politics and leaders.[11] National Socialism – or Nazism – was appealing because it encompassed a set of ideals, including 'the ideal of life as art, the cult of beauty, the fetishism of courage ... the family of man (under the parenthood of leaders).'[12] It was this apparently universal appeal that made fascism so dangerous.

Sontag's thesis offers a compelling theory as to the reasons why ordinary people like Gertrud Scholtz-Klink might have aligned themselves with the Nazi regime during the 1930s and early 1940s. Scholtz-Klink was one of thousands of women who joined the Nazi Party after Hitler's rise to power; it has been estimated that, of the 55,000 guards who worked at the concentration camps, approximately 10 per cent were female, and women worked in other sectors of Nazi life too. Scholtz-Klink was exceptional, however, in being the first to reach the position of Reich's Women's Führerin and then head of the Nazi Women's League. Having joined the Nazi Party along with her husband, she had risen quickly through the ranks. She was ultimately responsible for promoting the Nazi Party through speeches and

---

11 Susan Sontag, 'Fascinating Fascism', *New York Review of Books* (6 February 1975), p. 8. Available at: https://campus.albion.edu/gcocks/files/2013/08/Fascinating-Fascism.pdf.
12 Sontag, 'Fascinating Fascism', p. 10.

other public appearances. Scholtz-Klink parroted Hitler's views on issues such as femininity, motherhood and childbearing, arguing that the mission of all women in Nazi Germany was to tend to the needs of their fathers, husbands and sons. In a strange and rather self-defeating statement, she extolled the virtues of excluding women from the political scene: 'Anyone who has seen the Communist and Social Democratic women scream on the street and the parliament, realises that such an activity is not something which is done by a true woman.'[13] When the needs of the impending war required a shift in approach, Scholtz-Klink was appointed head of the Woman's Bureau in the German Labour Front and she was tasked with persuading women back into the workplace. When the regime collapsed, Scholtz-Klink escaped from Germany with her husband, although she was detained and imprisoned. Reflecting on her experiences in her book (written in 1978), Scholtz-Klink continued to advocate for the moral and political rectitude of Nazi ideology.

The enquiry 'Was Susan Sontag right about 'Fascinating Fascism'?' lends itself to a comparative analysis of fascist regimes and can serve well as a bridge between the examination of Hitler's Germany, Stalin's Russia and Mussolini's Italy. The rise of dictators is a popular topic at Key Stage 3, and this topic can be lent additional nuance when it draws upon the psychological insights of Sontag and others.

WHAT CAN WE LEARN FROM GERTRUD SCHOLTZ-KLINK ABOUT THE EXPERIENCES OF WOMEN IN NAZI GERMANY? (SIMILARITY AND DIFFERENCE)

This alternative enquiry question allows for particular focus on life under the Nazi regime and helps to fulfil GCSE specification points centred upon the experiences of ordinary Germans (including women, young people and minority groups). The enquiry makes visible some of the ways in which the Nazis indoctrinated ordinary Germans – although it does not seek to excuse Scholtz-Klink, nor to suggest that the followers of Nazism can be relieved of all responsibility for their activities.

In the enquiry, pupils begin by organising information relating to Scholtz-Klink's life into a target diagram. This is essentially a smaller circle nested inside a larger

---

13 John Simkin, 'Gertrud Scholtz-Klink', *Spartacus Educational* (September 1997). Available at: https://spartacus-educational.com/GERscholtz.htm.

one, both of which have been divided into three segments (like a clock face that has lines running from the 12 to the centre, from the 4 to the centre, and from the 8 to the centre). The three segments are labelled *Kinder* (children), *Küche* (kitchen) and *Kirche* (church) and pupils are asked to decide which segment to place each piece of information into: does it describe women's roles as mothers in Nazi society, women's work and responsibilities, or the beliefs and morals that women were supposed to possess? Once pupils have explored Scholtz-Klink's experiences, additional information is provided with an extra set of clues and pupils use a different coloured pen to transfer this evidence to their target grids.[14]

In my experience, pupils are endlessly fascinated by the ideological weight and reach of the Nazi regime; they find it difficult to comprehend, perhaps, why such abhorrent views were able to permeate all aspects of society, and they question the morality of ordinary Germans who seem to have been unmoved by the atrocities that were carried out around them. Of course, it is important that we complicate pupils' understanding of life in Nazi Germany by introducing them to the heroic men and women who resisted Nazi oppression, but we must also dwell on the stories of those who did not speak out – and who, in fact, helped to propagate the Nazi regime in a number of important ways. Sontag's thesis on the 'drama of the leader and the chorus' goes some way towards explaining the appeal of Nazi ideology for people like Gertrud Scholtz-Klink, but Scholtz-Klink's experiences – as well as those of millions of other men and women in Nazi Germany – underline the extent to which Nazi ideals simply came to embody the norm, offering inspiration and reassurance in the face of significant social, economic and political uncertainty.

KEY POINTS

- Gertrud Scholtz-Klink was a member of the Nazi Party, and after Hitler's rise to chancellor in 1933 she was made head of the Nazi Women's League.

- Scholtz-Klink promoted Hitler's views on women – first encouraging women to serve their fathers and husbands, and then later, as circumstances demanded, persuading them back to work.

---

14 For more on women in Nazi society, see Claudia Koonz, *Mothers in the Fatherland: Women, the Family and Nazi Politics* (London: Routledge, 1987).

- Susan Sontag's 'Fascinating Fascism' offers a framework according to which the notions of compulsion and fetishisation in fascist regimes can be explored.

- Scholtz-Klink's activities can also be used as a way of learning about life for ordinary people in Nazi Germany.

THE GRAND OLD LADY OF INDIAN INDEPENDENCE: ARUNA ASAF ALI

> ● **Suggested enquiry:** What should be included in a documentary about the life of Aruna Asaf Ali? (Significance)
>
> ● **Alternative enquiry:** How did the freedom fighter Aruna Asaf Ali contribute to the Indian independence movement? (Causation/Similarity and difference)

In August 1942, the Quit India movement – which demanded an end to British rule in India – was launched by the All India Congress Committee. Although Mahatma Gandhi's famous 'Quit India' speech set the tone for the campaign, with Gandhi famously appealing for his supporters to 'do or die', the important role played by Aruna Asaf Ali in the historic movement has often been overlooked.[15] It was Ali who chaired the meeting after some of the Committee's leaders had been arrested; it was Ali who raised the Congress flag at the Gowalia Tank Maidan (a park in central Mumbai), scorning the efforts of the police to shut down the session, even in the face of gunfire; and it was Ali who instigated a long-term underground movement agitating for Indian independence. Ali is remembered by many in India as a freedom fighter, and in several important ways she subverted expectations regarding the attitudes and approaches of (female) political activists in India.

Born into a Hindu Bengali family in the Punjab region of British India, Ali angered her parents when she decided to marry Asaf Ali, a member of the Indian National Congress Party (which demanded independence for India), and a Muslim more than twenty years her senior. Ali later described her family's reaction to her

---

15 Mahatma Gandhi, 'Quit India' speech, given at a meeting of the Congress in Bombay (August 1942). For further information see Lorraine Boissoneault, 'The Speech That Brought India to the Brink of Independence', *Smithsonian Magazine* (8 August 2017). Available at: https://www.smithsonianmag.com/history/speech-brought-india-brink-independence-180964366/.

marriage; many close family members disowned her, and Ali's uncle even performed the Śrāddha ritual for Ali, which was commonly used as a way of recognising those who had died. Ali joined the Indian National Congress and was first arrested on charges of vagrancy when she participated in the Salt March of 1930 (a non-violent protest against British taxation policies). A year after her release, she was once against taken into custody; this time she protested the poor treatment of political prisoners by going on hunger strike, which resulted in her being forced into solitary confinement. Ali's activities in 1942 again led to a warrant being issued for her arrest, but she went into hiding and a large reward was offered for her capture. After Indian independence was achieved, Ali joined the Communist Party of India and she became particularly involved in furthering the status and career opportunities for women in India. In 1958, she was elected the first mayor of Delhi and continued to campaign for improved education and working conditions until her death in 1997.[16]

WHAT SHOULD BE INCLUDED IN A DOCUMENTARY ABOUT THE LIFE OF ARUNA ASAF ALI? (SIGNIFICANCE)

Mahatma Gandhi's role in helping to bring about Indian independence often finds its way into Key Stage 3 schemes of work on decolonisation, although the part played by other individuals – especially women like Aruna Asaf Ali, Sarojini Naidu and Begum Rokeya – is less commonly explored. This significance enquiry helps pupils to develop an understanding of the ways in which Ali's story fits into the wider narrative of the Indian independence movement. It also spotlights the second-order concept of significance, as pupils determine the aspects of Ali's story that are most important, instructive or relevant for learning about the independence movement – and which, therefore, deserve to make the cut in a documentary that is to be made about the period.

Pupils begin by summarising chunks of information about Aruna Asaf Ali. If this information is presented in paragraph form in the middle column of a three-columned

---

16 Kuldip Singh, 'Obituary: Aruna Asaf Ali', *The Independent* (30 July 1996). Available at: https://www.independent.co.uk/news/people/obituary-aruna-asaf-ali-1331351.html. The obituary provides a useful overview of Ali's life and influence.

grid, pupils can use the column to the left of the information to assign each paragraph a title, and the column to the right to summarise each paragraph in two or three bullet points (a good way of checking that pupils have understood the information). Next, pupils are told that they must decide how much time they will devote to the different aspects of Ali's life and career in an hour-long documentary. The paragraphs that pupils have previously studied form the segments of the documentary, and pupils must apply significance criteria in deciding how many minutes to devote to each aspect. Which aspect of Ali's work had the most long-lasting impact? Which of her campaigns was the most resonant? How many people did she persuade to the cause at different points in her career? Finally, pupils record their decisions in the form of a pie chart (the sections of the pie representing minutes within the hour). Pupils add annotations to explain their reasoning.

Campaigns for freedom and political autonomy are rarely as monolithic as the term *movement* suggests; instead, they are pushed (sometimes nudged) forward by the actions of disparate individuals, whose approaches can sometimes appear contradictory and conflicting. India's independence movement was enacted by politicians, revolutionaries, poets and soldiers; some of those who campaigned for an independent Indian nation were exercised most strongly by the ideals of anti-colonialism and self-determination, whilst others had a socialist agenda and hoped to see India's farmers and labourers rise up against the land-owning zamindar class. An exclusive focus on the activities of Mahatma Gandhi does not do justice to the diversity of the struggle. Aruna Asaf Ali's story is important, therefore, in broadening and deepening pupils' understanding of the Indian independence movement, emphasising the extent to which power can sometimes be sited not in the hands of the few, but in the hands of the many.

KEY POINTS

- Aruna Asaf Ali was a key figure in the Indian independence movement.

- When a warrant was issued for her arrest, she went underground and continued to agitate for Indian independence.

- After India became independent in 1947, Ali focused on advancing political opportunities for women. She is recognised as a freedom fighter in India today.

- The second-order concept of significance can be explored using a plan-a-documentary activity.

Chapter 5
CONFLICT

Mir Dast, see page 123

INTRODUCTION

The theme of conflict tends to be well represented in the Key Stage 3 curriculum. The *History Programmes of Study* document makes reference to no less than nine different conflicts, ranging from the Hundred Years War and the Wars of the Roses (featured within the section on 'the development of Church, state and society in Medieval Britain 1066-1509') to the First and Second World Wars (examples specified within 'challenges for Britain, Europe and the wider world 1901 to the present day').[1] Warfare is a GCSE thematic unit option for the Assessment and Qualifications Alliance (AQA), Edexcel, Oxford, Cambridge and RSA Examinations (OCR) and the Welsh Joint Education Committee (WJEC), and at A level there is plenty of scope for pupils to consider the impact of various conflicts on the development of – for instance – British, Russian, Chinese and African societies. Often missing or neglected within these specifications or schemes of work, however, is the role played by individuals within broader military, political and ideological narratives – and, fundamentally, the contributions made by Black, Asian, minority ethnic groups and women to the development and resolution of conflict.

Recent academic work has highlighted the global nature of twentieth-century conflict: David Olusoga's *The World's War* outlines the experiences of Indian, African, Chinese and South-East Asian troops in World War One, and *Africa and World War II*, edited by Judith Byfield, Carolyn Brown, Timothy Parsons and Ahmad Alawad Sikainga, explores the significance of African arenas of conflict in World War Two.[2] Historians have also complicated traditional ideas concerning women's role in recent global conflicts, with work by Seema Shekhawat and Juliette Pattinson serving to underline the diverse nature of women's experiences.[3] However, it seems that traditional approaches to the delivery of lessons on, for example, World Wars One and Two remain common. Teachers tend to focus in the first instance on the more familiar Western (and largely male) arenas of war, before tackling other sites of conflict as an adjunct, including the typically feminised home front. A scarcity of readily available resources makes it even harder to shift

---

1 Department for Education, *History Programmes of Study: Key Stage 3 p. 2–4*.
2 David Olusoga, *The World's War: Forgotten Soldiers of Empire* (Croydon: Head of Zeus, 2014); Judith Byfield, Carolyn Brown, Timothy Parsons, Ahmad Alawad Sikainga (eds), *Africa and World War II* (Cambridge: Cambridge University Press, 2015).
3 Seema Shekhawat, *Female Combatants in Conflict and Peace* (London: Palgrave Macmillan, 2015); Juliette Pattinson, *Women of War: Gender, Modernity and the First Aid Nursing Yeomanry* (Manchester: Manchester University Press, 2020).

the delivery of lessons on earlier conflicts beyond a focus on the *central* arenas of battle or spaces of struggle.

The case studies in this section therefore offer opportunities for diversifying the teaching of conflicts including the French Revolution, the First World War, the Second World War and the Cold War. They foreground the experiences of individuals, moving away from the grand-narrative approach that tends to predominate in teaching (and thinking) about warfare and conflict. Ultimately, they help to convey the human impact of these global events, reaffirming the agency of individual soldiers, writers, nurses, resisters and spies.

THE REVOLUTIONARY POLITICS OF GERMAINE DE STAËL

- **Suggested enquiry:** Why was the novelist Germaine de Staël exiled from France in 1803? (Causation)
- **Alternative enquiry:** What impact did Germaine de Staël have on the French Revolution? (Consequence/Significance)

I first came across Germaine de Staël when I was researching the experiences of the late eighteenth century literati on the Grand Tour (a trip to see Europe most impressive historical sites, taken by young men and women keen to broaden their horizons). De Staël's appreciation of classical forms led her to view at least one performance by Emma Hamilton, who imitated ancient characters and statues for her husband William Hamilton's expatriate audiences in Naples (see page 151). De Staël wrote favourably of the performances, and perhaps even based the title character of her novel *Corinne, or Italy* upon Hamilton.[4] However, there was a good deal more to de Staël than this snapshot suggests. De Staël was a political theorist and intellectual; her books, travel writings and political tracts made a lasting impression on European thought and culture, and her revolutionary activities during the era of the French Revolution led first to her persecution by Napoleon, and later to her 10-year enforced exile from France.

Born in 1766, de Staël's father was Jacques Necker, a finance minister to King Louis XVI, who attracted the approbation of royalists when he introduced reforms aimed at reducing the Crown's debts. Her mother organised salons (gatherings of the well-to-do, and important sites for the exchange of ideas) which were attended by key Enlightenment figures including Voltaire and Diderot, and de Staël herself developed important connections with European writers and dignitaries. Despite her privileged background, de Staël was far from a monarchist; in her 1818 book *Considerations on the Principal Events of the French Revolution*, she described the

---

4   Germaine de Staël, *Corinne, or Italy*, tr. Isabel Hill (London: Richard Bentley, 1847).

excesses of the French kings and explained that the most effective form of government would be one based on popular sovereignty, representative government and respect for private property. De Staël also became a strong opponent of Napoleon's, comparing his character with that of Machiavelli.[5] Napoleon attacked de Staël for encouraging women to be too progressive, noting that she 'teaches people to think who had never thought before, or who had forgotten how to think.'[6] When de Staël helped to shelter Jean Gabriel Peltier (who plotted the death of Napoleon), Napoleon exiled de Staël without trial and for 10 years she was forbidden from returning to France. In 1814, an onlooker observed that 'there are three group powers struggling against Napoleon for the soul of Europe: England, Russia, and Madame de Staël'.[7] De Staël died in 1817, although the ideas and values she had expressed continued to influence writers and theorists well into the nineteenth century.

WHY WAS THE NOVELIST GERMAINE DE STAËL EXILED FROM FRANCE IN 1803?

This enquiry might see pupils organise information about de Staël into chronological order, allowing them to explore (or perhaps revisit, depending on where the enquiry is situated within the topic) the revolutionary events of late eighteenth- and nineteenth-century France. Next, pupils create a living graph determining the extent to which de Staël enjoyed favour or disapprobation at various points during her life. I like to do this activity using a card sort, giving pupils a range of cards (printed on white paper) that can be arranged in discussion with a partner on the desk (the higher the card, the greater the disapprobation experienced by de Staël). Then, a further set of cards can be distributed; these should be printed on a different colour and describe broader events in France. Pupils layer these on top of the first set of cards, allowing them to appreciate the relationships between events in

---

5   Germaine de Staël, *Considerations on the Principal Events of the French Revolution* (New York: James Eastburn & Co., 1818). Available at: https://oll-resources.s3.us-east-2.amazonaws.com/oll3/store/titles/2212/Stael_1459.html.

6   The Connexion, 'A Short History of Gemaine de Staël' (15 December 2020). Available at: https://www.connexionfrance.com/Mag/Culture/A-short-history-of-Germaine-de-Stael-whose-ideas-laid-the-foundations-of-Romanticism-and-female-emancipation#:~:text='She%20teaches%20people%20to%20think,written%20by%20Madame%20de%20Sta%C3%ABl. For a biography of de Staël, see Biancamaria Fontana, *Germaine de Staël: A Political Portrait* (Princeton, NJ: Princeton University Press, 2016).

7   The Connexion, 'A Short History of Germaine de Staël'.

de Staël's life and those in Revolutionary France. Pupils will note, for example, that de Staël was exiled in 1803 – and that the year of her exile coincided with the beginning of the Napoleonic Wars. Clearly, Napoleon was trying to rid the country of any destabilising influences at a time when he felt most under threat from within.

Finally, pupils might be asked to respond to the enquiry question. An interesting way of doing this is to provide pupils with a sheet featuring images of several individuals whose lives intersected with de Staël's; next to each of the images might be an empty speech bubble that pupils can use to outline why (according to the individual depicted) de Staël was exiled from France in 1803. The activity encourages pupils to place themselves in the shoes of people like Napoleon, Jacques Necker, Jean Gabriel Peltier and de Staël herself, and to summarise these individuals' interpretations. It is a useful means by which to emphasise the multifaceted nature of causation, and the extent to which explanation or justification for an event can often be highly contingent upon context and interpretation.

De Staël's story exemplifies the extent to which ordinary men and women could be caught up in revolutionary events and monumental conflicts – and, in de Staël's case, the galvanising impact of these broader narratives on an individual's writings and ideas. It also highlights the precarious nature of privilege and the volatility of life in Revolutionary France at a time when old certainties were being dismantled in the most violent of ways. De Staël's story deserves its place in any scheme of work on the French Revolution, providing an alternative lens through which to view this turbulent episode in European history.

KEY POINTS

- Germaine de Staël was a writer and political theorist who – despite her noble birth – argued for moderation, and an end to the excesses of the pre- and post-Revolutionary eras.

- De Staël was active in opposing Napoleon's tyrannical rule.

- In 1803, de Staël was exiled from France without trial.

- Examining the events of de Staël's life alongside those taking place in Revolutionary France helps pupils understand the impact of broader events on the lives of ordinary people.

BUFFALO CALF ROAD WOMAN

- **Suggested enquiry:** How did Indigenous Americans resist US government control? (Significance)

- **Alternative enquiry:** How damaging was westward expansion for Indigenous American ways of life? (Change and continuity)

The American West is a captivating topic, with its heroic cowboys, tenacious gold diggers and epic gunfighters. Americans today have much to thank the pioneering settlers for; on their march westward, these settlers established new towns and transport networks, laying the foundations for modern-day systems of justice, law and order, federal government and even methods of cattle ranching. Conflict between the settlers and the Indigenous Americans who inhabited the Great Plains forms a key component of the American West topic, although there is a tendency to present the Indigenous Americans in opposition to the settlers: whilst the settlers were innovative, the Indigenous Americans were traditional; and whilst the settlers were pioneering, the Indigenous Americans were somewhat timeless, with generation after generation relying on the land and the buffalo to ensure its survival. It is possible, too, that pupils might come away from a unit or scheme of work on the American West with the impression that the Indigenous Americans represented the enemy, blocking the enterprising migrants at every turn – and undertaking rather barbaric exploits (such as the infamous scalping of enemy skulls) in their efforts to prevent the inexorable, even divinely ordained progress of the settlers.

The story of Buffalo Calf Road Woman offers an opportunity to humanise the Indigenous Americans and to present the conflict between American settlers and the Indigenous Americans from the perspective of the colonised. Buffalo Calf Road Woman belonged to the Cheyenne group of Indigenous Americans. Today, the Cheyenne people have been split into two groups that are legally recognised by the US Bureau of Indian Affairs: the Southern Cheyenne (who live in Oklahoma) and the Northern Cheyenne (who live in Montana). In the mid-nineteenth century, the Cheyenne lived in modern-day North Dakota and South Dakota. The Cheyenne hold on the land was being steadily eroded, and in the 1870s gold was discovered in land that had recently been set aside for an Indigenous American reservation. When the government ordered representatives from the Cheyenne and Lakota groups to meet on the reservation to renegotiate sale of the land to the government, the Cheyenne did not comply and conflict broke out. The ensuing Battle of the Rosebud saw US government forces (led by the appropriately named General Crook) make significant advances through the Cheyenne and Lakota lines. The Indigenous Americans were in full retreat, their injured leaders laying sprawled on the battlefield, when Buffalo Calf Road Woman rode out and snatched up Chief Comes in Sight (her brother), dragging him to safety. Buffalo Calf Road Woman's actions not only saved her brother's life but had the effect of rallying the Cheyenne and Lakota forces, who went on to defeat General Crook's army. In a 2005 recounting of the group's oral history, contemporary Cheyenne storytellers described Buffalo Calf Road Woman's actions in subsequent battles, claiming that she had been the one to knock General Custer off his horse in the infamous Custer's Last Stand (1876).[8]

HOW DID INDIGENOUS AMERICANS RESIST US GOVERNMENT CONTROL? (SIGNIFICANCE)

Buffalo Calf Road Woman is deserving of historical study not just because of her heroic actions, but because of the important place that she has clearly come to assume in the oral traditions of the Cheyenne people. Her story can be featured within an enquiry focused on the ways in which Indigenous Americans resisted relocation at the hands of the US government. The enquiry might begin with a photograph of one of the t-shirts widely available for online sale, which depicts a band of Indigenous Americans in military-style garb underneath the caption 'Homeland Security: Fighting terrorism since 1492'.[9] Pupils can speculate about the significance of the date, before it is revealed to them that this was the year in which explorer Christopher Columbus landed in North America, kickstarting the colonisation of the Americas by various European powers. Pupils then spend time unpicking the term *terrorism*. Some pupils might be surprised by the term's usage;

---

8 Randy Salars, 'The Mystery of Buffalo Calf Road Woman', *Medium* (27 August 2021). Available at: https://medium.com/illumination/the-mystery-of-buffalo-calf-road-woman-c6174f26288f.
9 See https://www.britishmuseum.org/collection/object/E_2012-2017-4.

it is more readily used to describe the actions of modern-day radicals, and they might question its application in relation to the cattle ranchers, gold prospectors and cowboys who made their homes on America's Great Plains. However, when the historical reality of the US government actions is made clear to them, pupils might recognise the term's appositeness.

Pupils can then read short descriptions of the actions of Buffalo Calf Road Woman and other Indigenous American resisters. To help pupils digest the information, it is useful for them to summarise each sentence or paragraph in their own words: having to summarise content in, for example, ten to fifteen words is a great way of ensuring that the most important information has been understood. Pupils could then dual code the information (turn it into images or cartoons) to demonstrate a further level of understanding.

There are different ways in which pupils could apply their new knowledge. They might formulate thermometer judgements on the extent to which they agree with certain statements, for example: 'The Indigenous Americans were justified in their actions'. Alternatively, pupils might be asked to write letters to the creators of the 'Homeland Security' t-shirts, explaining the accuracy of the t-shirt's messages.

Ultimately, the enquiry helps to lend agency and individuality to the Indigenous Americans, deepening pupils' understanding of the ways in which Indigenous Americans resisted the seemingly inevitable onslaught on their ways of life in the course of the nineteenth century.

KEY POINTS

- Conflict between the US government and Indigenous Americans was frequent in the nineteenth century as the US government encouraged settlement on Indigenous American land.

- Buffalo Calf Road Woman was a Cheyenne woman who saved her wounded brother (Chief Comes in Sight) during the Battle of the Rosebud (1876).

- Buffalo Calf Road Woman features prominently within the oral history tradition of the modern-day Cheyenne.

- The enquiry underlines the concerted efforts at resistance undertaken by Indigenous Americans.

BROTHERS IN ARMS: MIR MAST AND MIR DAST

- **Suggested enquiry:** How were the lives of Mir Mast and Mir Dast affected by the First World War? (Significance)

- **Alternative enquiry:** Why did Mir Mast defect to the German army in 1915? (Causation)

In early November 1914, Ottoman sultan Mehmed V formally declared jihad (holy war) against the Entente Powers of World War One. Addressing a distinguished audience at Istanbul's Fatih Mosque, Mehmed claimed that Britain, France and Russia had long harboured 'ill-will against our great Caliphate', and millions of Muslims had suffered under these powers' 'tyranny'. He urged his army and navy to fight 'as lions' for 'the life and existence of both our country and 300 million Muslims.'[10] With this, Mehmed signalled the Ottoman Empire's entry into the First World War on the side of the Axis Powers, and the intention of the Ottomans to incite revolt and revolution amongst Muslim populations of enemy-held lands.

The arenas of war into which the Ottomans subsequently poured their troops deserve a more prominent place within our teaching of World War One, not least because of the role they played in such events as the breakdown of the Ottoman Empire, the abolition of the Ottoman Caliphate and the Armenian genocide. One way in which we might make the grand narrative of the Ottoman war effort more personal is to introduce pupils to the story of Mir Mast, a British-Indian soldier who defected to the German side – and whose own brother, extraordinarily, received high commendation for his efforts on behalf of the British. The experiences of these brothers – Mir Mast and Mir Dast – can help pupils to appreciate the significant geographical and demographic reach of the war and the diverse ways in which ordinary soldiers responded to the opportunities, challenges and tragedies presented to them by this global war.

---

10 Olusoga, *The World's War*, pp. 204–205.

HOW WERE THE LIVES OF MIR MAST AND MIR DAST AFFECTED BY THE FIRST WORLD WAR? (SIGNIFICANCE)

Asking pupils to plot events from the brothers' lives on a graph offers an opportunity to underline the fundamental aberration which the outbreak of war represented for the brothers – as well as for millions of colonial or non-European soldiers. Mir Mast and Mir Dast were born in the village of Tirah (close to the border between modern-day Pakistan and Afghanistan) and enlisted in the British Indian Army during the 1890s. When war broke out, Mir Dast fought in the 57th Wilde's Rifles (Frontier Force) and was commended for his gallantry during the Second Battle of Ypres. Mir Mast, too, was posted to the front line in France. However, he and a number of colleagues deserted their camp at Neuve Chapelle, defecting to the German side. Mir Mast was subsequently sent by the German army on a diplomatic mission to Afghanistan, where his local knowledge was utilised in efforts to persuade the Emir of Afghanistan to commit support to the Germans, and to foment uprising against British colonial rule. Whilst Mir Dast received the Victoria Cross for his services to the British, Mir Mast was recognised by Kaiser Wilhelm with an Iron Cross for his (ultimately unsuccessful) efforts in Central Asia.[11]

Mir Mast's story allows us to explore the idea of individual agency in the context of a war in which soldiers tend to be dehumanised by the industrial nature of its death and destruction. Pupils therefore categorise a range of evidence – including British army records of his desertion and drawings Mir Mast made of Allied trench positions in an apparent effort to convince the Germans of his usefulness – before deciding on the most important motives for the actions. Historian David Olusoga (who features the story of Mir Mast in *The World's War*) suggests that Mir Mast's ultimate motivation may have simply been to plot a route back home; in this he was successful, with British service records noting that Mir Mast was back in Tirah by June 1916.[12] The story of Mir Mast therefore serves as an opportunity to discuss the ideas and attitudes of imperial subjects, and the ideological, religious and

---

11 Andrew T. Jarboe, *Indian Soldiers in World War I: Race and Representation in an Imperial War* (Lincoln, NE: University of Nebraska Press, 2021). Jarboe tells the story of the brothers in the context of an examination of the role played by Indian Army soldiers in the war.
12 Olusoga, *The World's War*, pp. 242–243.

political allegiances (or perhaps the lack of such allegiances) that ordinary soldiers felt towards either their British or German masters.

The experiences of Mir Mast and Mir Dast can be used as the lens through which to explore other aspects of the war. Records from the 57th Wilde's Rifles can help pupils draw inferences and participate in discussion about the strategies and tactics used in the war, the treatment of troops on the front line, the wartime experiences of colonial soldiers and the diverse composition of infantry regiments.

Ultimately, the jihad which Mir Mast was tasked with helping to incite came to nothing; the Emir of Afghanistan refused to commit his support to the Germans and, indeed, the anticipated uprisings and revolutions by Muslim populations across British and French-held territories did not really materialise – at least not on the scale envisaged by Mehmed V and the German Kaiser. However, the movement was only really in its infancy in the years 1914–1918. As Italian writer Leone Caetani concluded in *The Times* as early as 1919, 'The entire Oriental world, from China to the Mediterranean, is in ferment. Everywhere the hidden fire of anti-European hatred is burning.'[13] Anti-colonial struggles were to manifest themselves in further jihadist movements of the twentieth and twenty-first centuries, and the legacies of these early stirrings were to be felt in the development of nationalist and funda-mentalist ideologies across the region. The story of Mir Mast helps pupils to grasp the ongoing resonance of this aspect of the war, as they are introduced to some of the events that laid the foundations for disputes that continue to seethe today.

KEY POINTS

- Born close to the border between modern-day Pakistan and Afghanistan, Mir Mast and Mir Dast both enlisted in the British Indian Army during the 1890s.

- Mir Dast was decorated for his bravery during the Battle of Ypres, whilst Mir Mast defected to the German side and supported the Kaiser's projects in Central Asia.

- The stories of Mir Mast and Mir Dast provide an alternative lens through which pupils can explore aspects of the First World War.

- It is important that pupils understand the legacies of the war and the links to jihadist movements of the twentieth and twenty-first centuries.

---

13 Alp Yenen, 'Legacies of Jihad 100 Years after World War I', *Gingko Library* (14 November 2014). Available at: https://edoc.unibas.ch/40784/1/20180323110905_5ab4d24164d65.pdf.

FREDDIE OVERSTEEGEN AND THE DUTCH RESISTANCE

- **Suggested enquiry:** Why were the resistance activities of individuals like Freddie Oversteegen so important? (Consequence)

- **Alternative enquiry:** How did the Dutch teenager Freddie Oversteegen resist the Nazis? (Significance)

Born in the village of Schoten in northern Holland in 1925, Freddie Oversteegen was influenced by the leftist politics of her close family members. Freddie's mother Trijntje was scarred by the economic uncertainties of the Great Depression and developed a distrust for capitalism and its exploitation of the working classes; her uncle George was a known anarchist. Freddie and her older sister Truus became members of the AJC Arbeiders Jeugd Central (AJC), a socialist youth group that taught folk dance, music and camping from a distinctly working-class, socialist slant. The Oversteegens' biographer Tim Brady claims that on one occasion Trijntje was found to have hosted a leftist meeting in their apartment so, in consequence, the local welfare organisation refused to support the family with food stamps and a rent stipend. A police officer was called when Trijntje rallied against this decision, and when an officer tried to force Trijntje out of the office, Freddie kicked him in the shin and Truus jumped on him and bit him. After Hitler came to power in 1933, the Oversteegen family did not hesitate in offering shelter to communist and socialist refugees as these individuals fought their way out of Germany and tried to make it to the relative safety of Britain.[14]

When war broke out in 1939, it was clear that Holland was not going to be allowed to remain neutral in the manner that the country had done during the First World War. The Dutch were entirely unprepared for war, however, with insufficient military forces and an outdated defence strategy, and on 10 May 1940 Nazi forces invaded Holland. Five days later, the Dutch forces surrendered and the country

---

14 Tim Brady, *Three Ordinary Girls* (New York: Kensington Publishing, 2021), pp. 5–8.

came under Nazi occupation. The Oversteegen family responded to the Nazi invasion by distributing anti-Nazi newspapers and pamphlets. They had been sheltering Jewish refugees since Hitler's intentions regarding the Jews had become clear during the 1930s, and as the Nazis occupied their country, the family continued to take Jewish men, women and children into their home. In 1941, a commander from the Haarlem Resistance Group recruited Freddie and Truus and they began to carry out acts of sabotage, using dynamite to disable bridges and destroy railway tracks. As their status within the resistance movement grew – and as the people of Holland became evermore desperate to rid their country of the Nazi invaders – Freddie and Truus were entrusted with an even more dangerous task: to isolate and kill Nazi officers. Freddie was the first of the sisters to kill a soldier (she did so whilst riding her bicycle through Haarlem). The girls also lured soldiers to the local woods, approaching them in bars and taverns and asking them to accompany the girls for a stroll, before shooting and killing them. One of the sisters' friends, Hannie – a fellow saboteur – was caught and arrested in 1945; she was killed by the Nazis for her activities. This event contributed to the trauma experienced by Freddie and Truus in the post-war years, with both sisters reluctant to speak of the activities in which they had been involved for many years.[15]

WHY WERE THE RESISTANCE ACTIVITIES OF INDIVIDUALS LIKE FREDDIE OVERSTEEGEN SO IMPORTANT? (CONSEQUENCE)

This enquiry might begin with an overview of Oversteegen's story. I think it works well to carry this out through a decision-maker activity, presenting pupils with various choices and asking them how they would have reacted in some of the circumstances Oversteegen found herself in. For example, 'You have been hearing reports of Nazi atrocities for several years and Nazi soldiers have finally reached the borders of your country. They seem intent on invading and it is likely that, if successful, they would chip away at all freedoms of speech, expression and religion in the country. What would you do?' Other scenarios might see pupils asked

---

15 For an overview of Freddie Oversteegen's story, see Naomi O'Leary, '"Her War Never Stopped": The Dutch Teenager who Resisted the Nazis', *The Guardian* (23 September 2018). Available at: https://www.theguardian.com/world/2018/sep/23/freddie-oversteegen-dutch-teenager-who-resisted-nazis.

how they would have responded to the news of the Nazis' atrocities on the European continent, their occupation of Holland, the invitation to partake in sabotage and to increasing evidence of the treatment of Jewish people (and other groups) in the concentration camps. The activity is not intended to imply that all affirmative action is necessarily to be encouraged – nor, indeed, to suggest that Oversteegen's heroism was dependent on her participation in dangerous underground activities against the Nazis. Rather, the task highlights the extent to which the decisions undertaken by Oversteegen and many of her fellow resisters had to be taken in the moment, and there was very little opportunity to think through the ramifications of their actions.

Next, give pupils a radar graph template: the vertical line should be labelled *passive* (at the top) and *active* (at the bottom); and the horizontal line should be labelled *effective* (on the left) and *ineffective* (on the right). Pupils read more about the activities of Oversteegen, her sister and her friend Hannie, and they can plot this information onto the graph to indicate the extent to which these activities were passive or active, and effective or ineffective. Next, distribute short summaries of some of the other resistance activities carried out during the war, and ask pupils to plot these onto their radar graphs in the same way. Some of the activities might include: hiding Jewish men, women and children from the Nazis; espionage; assassination attempts; refusal to comply with the Nazis; strikes and demonstrations; raids; and uprisings. Sharing further instances of resistance during World War Two allows pupils to draw comparisons, and to place Oversteegen's activities within their proper context. Finally, pupils should be able to respond to the enquiry question, drawing upon their knowledge of Oversteegen and her colleagues' actions – as well as the sense of alarm engendered by the fast-paced decision-maker activity – to explain why Oversteegen's resistance activities were so significant.

Resisters are now recognised to have had a significant impact during the Second World War. Not only did they help to save many thousands of individuals from capture, imprisonment and execution, but they had an untold (and ultimately unmeasurable) importance in bolstering morale, undermining the actions and assertions of the Nazis and their supporters. Foregrounding the experiences of Freddie Oversteegen helps to emphasise the significant role played by ordinary individuals as they lived through era-defining events. It also helps pupils to appreciate the numerous ways in which it was possible to resist the Nazis, and the value of both overt and covert opposition in standing up to tyranny and oppression.

KEY POINTS

- Freddie Oversteegen was a Dutch resister during World War Two.

- She carried out acts of sabotage against Nazi occupiers, as well as murdering Nazi officers.

- By engaging pupils in a decision-maker activity, they are encouraged to recognise the pressure under which resisters were forced to act.

- Exploring different kinds of resistance activities helps pupils appreciate the multifaceted nature of opposition to Nazi occupation and oppression.

JAN FLISIAK AND THE POLISH UNDERGROUND RESISTANCE

- **Suggested enquiry:** What role did Jan Flisiak play in the Polish underground resistance during World War Two? (Significance)

- **Alternative enquiry:** How important was resistance and insurgence in bringing about an end to communist rule? (Significance/Change and continuity)

When Nazi troops invaded Poland on 1 September 1939 (marking the beginning of World War Two), Jan Flisiak was 18 years old. Flisiak was born in Lubartów (a small town not far from the historic city of Lublin in eastern Poland) and at the outbreak of the war he was working on a family farm, having just finished secondary school. Flisiak joined the resistance without hesitation; from January 1940 he was numbered amongst the ranks of the Związek Walki Zbrojnej (Union of Armed Struggle) – an underground army that resisted the occupation of Poland by both Nazi and Soviet forces – carrying out activities to weaken the occupying forces, as well as working to maintain Polish cultural traditions. To begin with, Flisiak's role was to distribute illegal leaflets amongst Polish citizens, spreading information and fortifying morale. However, he was soon assigned to the task of protecting the Union in a more direct way, hunting down traitors and collaborators and helping to enlist more soldiers to the ranks of the underground partisan group. He seems to have been known to the Gestapo from the middle of 1943, although Flisiak still managed to form his own partisan unit – known as the Chłopicki unit, in tribute to a nickname that Flisiak was himself given – of local men and women which carried out underground activities throughout the period.

In September 1944, Flisiak was arrested by the the Russian secret police (NKVD) and imprisoned in Lublin Castle where he was sentenced to death for his activities. However, Flisiak managed to escape from the castle along with ten other prisoners, and he went into hiding. The official end of the war in Europe in 1945 did not bring about the Polish independence desired by Flisiak and his fellow resisters. A communist-controlled government was established, with Stalin's sphere of influence (which included Poland) receiving something akin to official sanction by the Western powers in the Potsdam Conference of July 1945. Flisiak was one of an estimated 200,000 Poles involved in partisan warfare during the late 1940s and early 1950s, many of whom continued to fight for Polish independence in the face of oppression and – in some cases – violent atrocity committed by NKVD units stationed across the Polish territory. In a shootout between Flisiak's unit and members of the NKVD, Flisiak was shot in the stomach; he was arrested whilst receiving treatment at a hospital in Lublin and reinterned at the prison at Lublin Castle. Sentenced to life imprisonment, Flisiak died in March 1950 as a result of complications from tuberculosis. It was not until 1993 – the same year that the last post-Soviet troops left Poland – that all charges against Flisiak were dropped.[16]

I first came across Flisiak's story because he is an ancestor of my husband's. My brother-in-law has researched Flisiak's experiences and shared them with Polish veteran organisations, and when we go to Poland we often visit Flisiak's memorial. Understandably, communist history is important to many people in Poland and there is great interest in uncovering the contributions of people like Jan Flisiak to the underground resistance movement. Flisiak is, of course, just one of many individuals whose youth was shaped by the events of the 1940s and 1950s – but the fact that I can add so much personal colour to the retelling of Flisiak's experiences means that his story is one that earns its place in an enquiry focused on life in occupied Poland during the mid-twentieth century.

---

16 For an overview of Flisiak's story, see Anna Kister, 'Biographical Notes: Jan Flisiak', *Hieronim Dekutowski* (n.d.). Available at: https://www.hieronimdekutowski.pl/artykuly-znanych-autorow/ noty-biograficzne-jan-flisiak-ps-chlopicki/. This offers a useful biography, although the English translation is imperfect.

WHAT ROLE DID JAN FLISIAK PLAY IN THE POLISH UNDERGROUND RESISTANCE DURING WORLD WAR TWO? (SIGNIFICANCE)

This enquiry might begin with Flisiak's role in rallying support for the anti-communist cause, before zooming out to consider Flisiak's activities within the broader context of resistance and opposition to communist rule across Poland. Pupils read a summary of the actions undertaken by Flisiak and they are asked to pause at various points to summarise what they have read (in order to demonstrate their comprehension), rating the level of danger Flisiak found himself in. Next, pupils can explore other instances of opposition to communist rule in Poland, with case studies including military attacks on state security offices, acts of non-compliance within the gulag-style prison camps set up across Poland, and the political agitation organised by Solidarność, – the trade union founded by Lech Wałęsa and other anti-Soviet leaders in 1980. Pupils might be asked to rate the level of danger associated with each of these case studies, perhaps plotting their ideas onto a *danger-o-meter* (a speedometer template, with the red zone representing the highest level of danger).

Analysing political cartoons or propaganda posters can be a useful way of rounding off an enquiry like this, as it allows pupils to apply the knowledge they have gained to the task of deconstructing the images in question. In this case, there is an abundance of anti-communist sources from which to choose. However, a poster entitled 'Hej, kolenda, kolenda!' (produced during the late 1940s or early 1950s) would offer particularly fruitful opportunities for analysis.[17] The poster depicts Stalin as Father Christmas (or, literally, 'Grandpa Frost'), and to him is shackled Bolesław Bierut, the Polish politician who served in Poland's Soviet-controlled puppet government from 1947 until 1956. Loosely translated, the caption reads 'Beware Father Christmas and the red star regime'. Pupils could dissect the symbols and messages contained within this and other posters, applying their knowledge of Polish attitudes towards communist rule.

Flisiak's story is one that I learnt of through family research, but there are countless others whose acts of defiance can be used to exemplify resistance and insurgence – themes that can seem rather abstract unless they are personalised. With

---

17 See https://books.openedition.org/iheid/6649.

thousands of Polish-born children attending school in the UK, it is essential that we weave Polish history into our curricula – and that, where possible, we add nuance to this history by lingering upon the stories of real, ordinary Polish men and women from the past.

KEY POINTS

- Jan Flisiak was an underground resister during the period when the Nazis and the Soviets occupied Poland.

- Flisiak's work attempting to sabotage the occupiers got him in trouble with both the Gestapo and the NKVD. Ultimately, he was arrested and imprisoned by the NKVD.

- Flisiak's story provides a case study for the exploration of themes like resistance and occupation.

- Personal stories like Flisiak's can make the heroic feel more human.

SECRETS, SPIES AND A SAFEWAY BAG: OLEG GORDIEVSKY

- **Suggested enquiry:** How significant was the role played by spies during the Cold War? (Significance)

- **Alternative enquiry:** How did a Safeway bag and a Mars Bar help Oleg Gordievsky escape from the Committee for State Security (KGB)? (Evidential understanding)

Spy stories remain endlessly fascinating, and delivering lessons focused on the shadowy, death-defying and often implausible escapades of Cold War spies helps to enrich our teaching of the Second World War and post-war periods. Pupils are surprised to learn of the role played by Roald Dahl – creator of Oompa-Loompas, Muggle-Wumps and Twits – as he worked on behalf of the Secret Intelligence Service (MI6) to galvanise US support for the war; they are fascinated, too, by the efforts of Ursula Kuczynski, who famously passed on details of the Americans' nuclear testing programme, thus hastening the development of the Soviet Union's atomic bomb. However, the story of Oleg Gordievsky offers particularly fruitful opportunity for deepening pupils' understanding of the important work done by apparent bit players in turning the tides of international diplomacy and intelligence gathering. Indeed, though Gordievsky's significant role in Cold War-era espionage activities is unquestionable, there were a number of lesser-known individuals (many of them women) to whom Gordievsky owed his success and efficacy – and, probably, his life.

The son of a loyal NKVD officer, Oleg Gordievsky's family connections and intelligence earned him a trusted role in the secret service apparatus of Khrushchev's Russia. Gordievsky completed postings in East Berlin, Moscow and Copenhagen – however, the building of the Berlin Wall and the Soviet invasion of Czechoslovakia served to convince Gordievsky of Soviet corruption, and the Russian began to pass information to MI6. When Gordievsky was posted to the Soviet embassy in London, he discharged secrets from the innermost circles of the KGB to British handlers, who met Gordievsky monthly at a flat in Bayswater. Gordievsky's wife Leila – a KGB officer herself – was not aware of her husband's deception; indeed, when the truth of Gordievsky's defection came out many years later, the marriage effectively ended.

The story of Gordievsky's life as an undercover agent reads like the most compulsive of thrillers; the extent to which Gordievsky's survival depended on luck, circumstance and the hypervigilance of his handlers and co-conspirators almost beggars belief.[18] One of the most effective ways of conveying this to pupils is through a decision-maker activity in which pupils put themselves in Gordievsky's shoes, imagining how they themselves might have responded to the decisions that faced him. The activity gives pupils insight into the high-octane life of a Cold War spy.

HOW SIGNIFICANT WAS THE ROLE PLAYED BY SPIES DURING THE COLD WAR? (SIGNIFICANCE)

In order to delve more deeply into the significance of Gordievsky's activities in the context of Cold War politics, pupils are given packs of sources detailing the key events connected with Gordievsky's work. Pupils could employ any number of models to judge the significance of Gordievsky's actions, although the criteria outlined by Geoffrey Partington in his 1980 book *The Idea of an Historical Education* works especially well for this task.[19] Pupils would note, for example, that Gordievsky's actions had a profound impact as he convinced the British of Soviet anxiety surrounding a future nuclear strike and, perhaps, encouraged a rather more cautious approach to British–Soviet relations. Gordievsky's work also fulfilled Partington's criteria for durability as he remained active throughout the 1970s and 1980s (demonstrating a talent for self-preservation that was rare amongst Cold War-era spies).

---

18 Ben Macintyre, *The Spy and the Traitor* (London: Penguin, 2018). Macintyre describes the events of Gordievsky's life in detail; the book effectively conveys the thriller-like nature of Gordievsky's eventual escape from the KGB.

19 Geoffrey Partington, *The Idea of an Historical Education* (Slough: NFER Publishing Company, 1980), pp. 112–116.

One of the most memorable aspects of the Gordievsky story is the role played by periphery individuals in coordinating both Gordievsky's espionage activities and – perhaps most dramatically – in engineering his final escape. Valerie Pettit, for example, has recently been disclosed as the MI6 officer who masterminded Operation Pimlico: the ambitious plan to extricate Gordievsky from the clutches of the KGB – a plan which, brilliantly, hinged upon Gordievsky being spotted on a particular street corner in Moscow, carrying a Safeway bag and eating a Mars Bar as a signal of his need to be spirited away. Similarly, the wife of MI6 station chief Roy Ascot, Caroline, saved Gordievsky from certain exposure whilst Gordievsky was smuggled to safety across the Finnish border, using the smell of her baby's soiled nappy to distract sniffer dogs who were taking an interest in the boot of the Ascots' Ford saloon.

The contributions of such individuals can be explored through a significance enquiry in which pupils perhaps consider how Valerie Pettit/MI6 handlers ought to be commemorated. Pupils can consider evidence relating to these individuals' roles, perhaps exploring counterfactual scenarios hinging upon the supposed fail-ure of Gordievsky's operations. Finally, they could produce a suitable method for commemorating Pettit, Ascot and others, perhaps in the form of a plaque, a statue or a textbook spread in which the importance of these often-overlooked individu-als is foregrounded.

KEY POINTS

- The son of an NKVD officer, Oleg Gordievsky defected to the British side during the 1970s.

- Gordievsky passed information to MI6, playing a key role in Cold War-era politics.

- Gordievsky's escape from the clutches of the KGB in Operation Pimlico depended on a Safeway bag and the soiled remains of a baby's nappy.

- Gordievsky's story can be used within a significance enquiry on the role of Cold War-era espionage.

Emma Hamilton, see page 151

Chapter 6
SOCIETY AND CULTURE

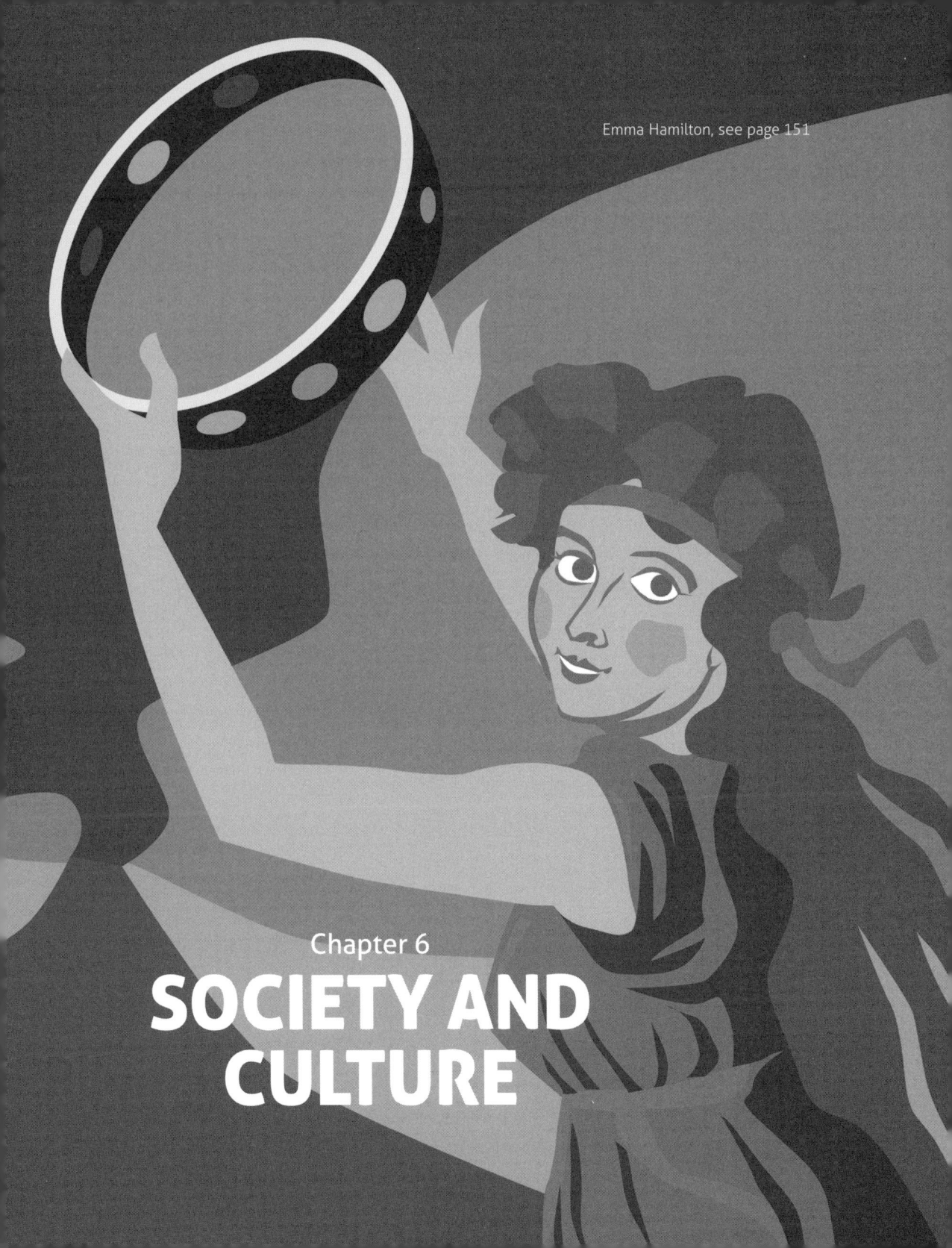

INTRODUCTION

Historians of gender, sexuality and culture have had a significant impact on academic history since the 1960s, challenging the traditional focus on political and military history, and instigating more nuanced examination of female, lesbian, gay, transgender and bisexual identities, as well as extending investigation beyond elite and/or royal power to the working classes.

The extent to which these approaches have been adopted at a secondary-school level has been mixed. Whilst the 2013 *History Programmes of Study: Key Stage 3* document stipulated that pupils ought to 'gain historical perspective by placing their growing knowledge into different contexts, understanding the connections between ... cultural, economic, political, religious and social history', the realisation of this aim is not straightforward.[1] Social and cultural history can feel rather auxiliary to the topics delivered at Key Stage 3 – partly because, it seems, they are often separated (in our enquiry questions and in the activities we plan) from the events to which they relate. When the document indicates, for example, that pupils ought to learn about the 'development of Church, state and society in Medieval Britain 1066–1509', it is suggested that one topic to support this is 'the Black Death and its social and economic impact': the phrasing of this recommendation gives the impression that pupils will need to learn first about the Black Death before going on to explore its social and economic impact – as though the two are separate.[2] A similar problem may arise when it is suggested that pupils learn about 'social, cultural and technological change in post-war British society' as part of their exploration of 'challenges for Britain, Europe and the wider world 1901 to the present day'.[3] This might be interpreted as a recommendation to first deliver lessons on the *big events* (such as the First and Second World Wars and the end of empire), before then exploring the social and cultural changes that occurred in consequence of these developments.

Social and cultural histories are best viewed not as incidental aspects of the topics we deliver, but as lenses through which we might actually teach these topics. With this in mind, a social- or cultural-history approach has been used to frame the case studies in this section. The stories have been selected because they offer insight

---

1 Department for Education, *History Programmes of Study: Key Stage 3*, p. 2.
2 Department for Education, *History Programmes of Study: Key Stage 3*, pp. 2–3.
3 Department for Education, *History Programmes of Study: Key Stage 3*, p. 4.

into, variously, female, working-class, disability or transgender experience in their particular period or context. They are also intended to reflect and underline the diversity of human experience – an acknowledgement of which is at the heart of social and cultural history. Several of the case studies are connected to popular entertainment as, in my view, this approach not only lends itself to the delivery of engaging lessons (due to the availability of interesting contemporary sources), but it fosters insight into the experiences, tastes and concerns of real people in the past.

BLACK LUCE, OR SHAKESPEARE'S DARK LADY

> ● **Suggested enquiry:** What can we learn from Black Luce and other Black Tudors about diversity in Elizabethan England? (Significance)
>
> ● **Alternative enquiry:** What can Shakespeare's Dark Lady tell us about race relations in the sixteenth century? (Significance/Change and continuity)

In Sonnet 127 – the first of his so-called Dark Lady Sonnets – William Shakespeare wrote, 'In the old age black was not counted fair, / Or if it were, it bore not beauty's name; / But now is black beauty's successive heir, / And beauty slandered with a bastard shame'. Shakespeare went on to describe the 'mistress' in question, noting the 'raven black' of her eyes and the 'black wires' that grew on her head – and concluding 'Thy black is fairest in my judgment's place'.[4] The identity of Shakespeare's Dark Lady has been the subject of considerable speculation, with some historians suggesting that Shakespeare might have been inspired by a real woman of African descent – perhaps a woman known as Black Luce, who might have met Shakespeare around the time of the first performance of *Twelfth Night*.[5] Whether or not the identity of the Dark Lady is ever confirmed, Shakespeare's depiction affords valuable insight into contemporaries' attitudes towards Black men and women. The story of Black Luce also contributes to the project – inspired by the work of historians like Miranda Kauffman – whereby the Black presence in Tudor England is exposed, and the presumption that Black Tudors must necessarily have been enslaved, exploited or downtrodden is challenged.[6]

Close reading of Shakespeare's Dark Lady Sonnets is a good place to start the enquiry – and promote the key interdisciplinary skill of close, analytical reading. Pupils ought to explore the language used to convey the poet's admiration

---

4   See https://shakespeare.folger.edu/shakespeares-works/shakespeares-sonnets/sonnet-127/.
5   For example, see George Bagshawe Harrison, *Shakespeare under Elizabeth* (New York: H. Holt & Co, 1933), p. 64.
6   Miranda Kauffman, *Black Tudors: The Untold Story* (London: Oneworld Publications, 2017).

(perhaps even infatuation) with the Dark Lady. They might identify Shakespeare's reflections on the nature of beauty and purity, and speculate on the extent to which it is possible to find literal meaning in his words; was Shakespeare making reference to an individual with whom he himself was acquainted? Or was he merely setting up the blackness (i.e. perhaps evil, or metaphorical darkness) of the Dark Lady as a juxtaposition to his famous Fair Youth?

Little is known of the real figure upon whom Shakespeare might have based his Dark Lady. Historian George Bagshawe Harrison indicates that Black Luce was the name of a Clerkenwell brothel owner – and Harrison tentatively suggests that Shakespeare might have encountered this individual in around 1601–1602.[7] Beyond this, however, we have limited information about her life. Yet the story of Black Luce can be combined with fragments from the lives of other Black Tudors to help tell the story of social diversity in sixteenth-century England.

WHAT CAN WE LEARN FROM BLACK LUCE AND OTHER BLACK TUDORS ABOUT DIVERSITY IN ELIZABETHAN ENGLAND? (SIGNIFICANCE)

Pupils are asked to read portions of text taken from Kauffman's *Black Tudors*, and to summarise their findings about individuals including John Blanke (the royal trumpeter who was richly rewarded for his work at Henry VIII's Westminster Tournament in 1511), Mary Fillis (a seamstress working in Smithfield in the late sixteenth century) and Diego (a formerly enslaved man who escaped Spanish ser-vitude to join Francis Drake's voyages of discovery in the 1570s). These case studies serve to complicate notions about the Black presence in Tudor England, positing individuals like Blanke, Fillis and Diego (as well as the *real* Black Luce) as ordinary men and women living and working in Tudor society.

Having engaged with these case studies, pupils use their new knowledge to respond to certain statements (which serve to test the extent to which they have understood the readings). I use activities like thermometer or speedometer judge-ments to help pupils with their evaluations; these help to promote the idea that historical judgements are very rarely a simple case of *agree* and *disagree*. Pupils

---

7   George Bagshawe Harrison, *Shakespeare under Elizabeth* (New York: H. Holt & Co, 1933), p. 64.

decide, for example, how accurate the following statements are: 'Most Black men and women in Tudor England came directly from Africa', 'The majority of Africans living in England were poor' and 'Africans living in England made up only a small percentage of the population'. Pupils are encouraged to annotate their thermometers or speedometers with evidence, to justify the decisions they have made.

I have started teaching the new Migrants in Britain (Edexcel) GCSE course this academic year and it has been interesting to explore some of pupils' deep-seated notions about life and diversity in early modern England. Many pupils are, I think, very knowledgeable about the Tudors; they can certainly recount an impressive amount of information about the monarchs and their spouses, and their understanding of the tumultuous religious changes of the period is strong, too. However, they do maintain rather narrow, uncomplicated views about ordinary life and social demographics during the period. An enquiry that adds nuance to pupils' understanding of diversity in Tudor England therefore earns its place in Key Stage 3, Key Stage 4 and even Key Stage 5 schemes of work. It is important that we help pupils to recognise the extent to which Black men and women formed part of the fabric of ordinary life during the period – and that, according to the evidence offered in baptism records, tournament rolls and shipping accounts, they were accepted and integrated into society (despite Shakespeare's problematic *othering* of the Black body in his famous sonnets). Racially informed discrimination and division were intertwined with the slave trade, but the Black presence in England predated the emergence of this invidious enterprise – and Black Tudors form an important, yet often neglected part of Britain's multicultural past.

KEY POINTS

- Shakespeare's Dark Lady Sonnets featured a woman of African descent; she was described as having 'raven black' eyes and 'black wires' on her head.

- Shakespeare might have been inspired by a real African woman: Black Luce, the owner of a brothel in Clerkenwell.

- Shakespeare's Dark Lady can be woven into an enquiry focused on diversity in Tudor England.

- It is important to individualise men and women of African descent living in Tudor England, and extracts from Miranda Kauffman's book *Black Tudors* can help with this.

PETER THE WILD BOY

- **Suggested enquiry:** What can we learn from Peter the Wild Boy about attitudes towards disability in the eighteenth century? (Significance)

- **Alternative enquiry:** How much did the treatment of disabled men and women change during the eighteenth and nineteenth centuries? (Change and continuity)

In 1725, a young boy was found – naked and alone – in the woods near Hamelin, Hanover. He appeared to have been living a wild existence as he walked on all fours and did not communicate verbally. By coincidence, those who had found the boy were from a hunting party organised by King George I (who had been visiting his homeland). George seemed to have been encouraged by his daughter-in-law, Caroline of Ansbach, to adopt the boy and he was taken to Britain – where he was transformed into a curiosity, or human pet, for those at court to gape at. Peter was the subject of a book by author Jonathan Swift called *The Most Wonderful Wonder that Ever Appeared to the Wonder of the British Nation.*[8] The book focuses on an imagined dialogue between Peter and a bear (supposedly the boy's foster mother), and mocked the British for their obsession with him. Daniel Defoe also described Peter in a 1726 book called *Mere Nature Delineated*, concluding that he was 'all wild, brutal, and as soul-less as he was said to be; acting mere nature, and little more than a vegetative life; dumb, or mute, without the least appearance of cultivation, or of having ever had the least glympse [sic] of conversation among the rational part of the world.'[9] Attempts to educate Peter failed, and when those at court tired of him, he was handed over to the care of a servant woman who installed Peter into a farmhouse in Northchurch, Hertfordshire. A collar with Peter's name and address was made for him in case he went missing, and Peter seems to have lived until he was around 70. When he died, locals paid for a headstone and the grave now boasts Grade II listing following a recommendation made by English Heritage in 2013.

---

8   Jonathan Swift, *The Most Wonderful Wonder that Ever Appeared to the Wonder of the British Nation* (London: G. Faulkner, 1726).
9   Daniel Defoe, *Mere Nature Delineated* (London: T. Warner, 1726), p. 3.

Analysis by historians and medical professionals suggests that Peter might have had a rare genetic condition known as Pitt-Hopkins Syndrome. A portrait of Peter by the Georgian court painter William Kent depicts him with hooded eyelids and a Cupid's bow mouth; these facial features can be indicative of the syndrome which is sometimes also associated with autism, sensory disorders and cognitive impairment.[10] Pitt-Hopkins Syndrome was only identified in 1978. At the time, Peter was presumed simply to have been feral, and observation of his behaviours was seized upon as an opportunity for understanding the supposed differences between the natural and human worlds. For many, Peter was the antithesis of humanity, reason and progress; he was a creature entirely incapable of advancement, according to the ideals of the Enlightenment era.

WHAT CAN WE LEARN FROM PETER THE WILD BOY ABOUT ATTITUDES TOWARDS DISABILITY IN THE EIGHTEENTH CENTURY? (SIGNIFICANCE)

This enquiry might first explore the contemporary responses to Peter. Pupils can undertake close analysis of extracts from the writings of Swift and Defoe, as well as an anonymous pamphlet called *An Enquiry how the Wild Youth, Lately Taken in the Woods Near Hanover*, reports from George I's courtiers, and the parish register of Northchurch, which described the circumstances leading to Peter's arrival in Hertfordshire.[11] Pupils identify some of the language used to exoticise, infantilise and dehumanise Peter through reference, for example, to his apparent lack of civilisation, and to the inappropriate behaviour and the inadequate decorum he showed when brought before the court. Pupils might note the irrationality of some of the failings attributed to Peter. For example, he once mischievously seized the Lord Chamberlain's staff of office and hat, and put them on before an audience with the king; this behaviour was considered evidence of Peter's bestiality, although today we might note the absurdity of a court protocol that prohibited this minor practical joke. Ultimately, pupils should come to recognise the concerted

---

10 For a mezzotint after William Kent's painting, see https://www.npg.org.uk/collections/search/portrait/mw38145/Peter-the-Wild-Boy.

11 Anon., *An Enquiry how the Wild Youth, Lately Taken in the Woods Near Hanover* (London: H. Parker, 1726). For other sources, see Lucy Worsley, 'Peter the Wild Boy', *The Public Domain Review* (7 November 2011). Available at: https://publicdomainreview.org/essay/peter-the-wild-boy.

efforts made by Peter's observers to portray Peter as fundamentally different – as contemporaries strove to enact a clear division between the civilised/enlightened and the uncivilised/unenlightened (with Peter serving to embody the characteristics of the latter).

It is important that Peter's experiences are placed within the context of broader attitudes towards disability in the eighteenth century, so pupils might go on to explore evidence relating to the treatment of other mental and physical impairments and disabilities in the Georgian period.[12] They might examine some of the innovative methods and aids designed to help blind and disabled people move and work (such as the wooden contraptions designed to propel disabled people through the streets, earning disabled men and women the nickname 'billies in bowls'). They could explore the work of the Foundling Hospital in Bloomsbury, London, which was set up in 1739 and helped blind children by teaching them to play musical instruments; and they might also study the careers of disabled artists such as Sampson Towgood Roch and Joshua Reynolds. Of course, pupils ought to also examine the significant struggles faced by disabled men, women and children in Georgian England – and the tragic frequency with which disability resulted in ostracism, discrimination and destitution.

A curriculum cannot be truly representative if it does not make room for the study of disability. Pupils should be made aware of the experiences of individuals who suffered as a result of limited understanding and medical knowledge in the past – as well as the experiences of those who overcame significant challenges and hardship. Peter's story helps to humanise the historical study of disability, as well as providing an alternative lens through which to investigate this period of supposed progress and enlightenment in British history.

KEY POINTS

- Peter was a young boy found naked and alone in the woods near Hanover, Germany in 1725.

- He was brought to England by King George I and became a curiosity, or human pet, before being discarded once interest in him waned.

---

12 See David Turner, *Disability in Eighteenth-Century England* (Abingdon: Routledge, 2012). This book provides a comprehensive overview of attitudes towards disability in Britain during the eighteenth century.

- Peter is now thought to have had a genetic condition known as Pitt-Hopkins Syndrome; this helps to explain his physical characteristics and behaviours.

- Study of mental and physical disability is an essential aspect of a diverse and representative curriculum.

AN ABSURD HERO(INE): THE CHEVALIER D'EON

- **Suggested enquiry:** What does the story of the Chevalier d'Eon tell us about ideas of gender in the eighteenth century? (Significance)

- **Alternative enquiry:** Was the Chevalier d'Eon really a strange case in the Enlightenment era? (Similarity and difference)

The story of the Chevalier d'Eon introduces pupils to the history of gender – and it does so through the lens of the Enlightenment, allowing for this study of gender to be grounded within a recognisable historical framework. D'Eon's story serves to challenge the notion of transsexuality as a recently conceived marker of identity, highlighting contemporary discussions of gender identity as rather less modern than pupils might imagine.

Born Charles d'Eon de Beaumont, the Chevalier d'Eon was to assume a dizzying number of identities in the course of his lifetime. He was educated in the law, and first attracted the attention of French society as an acute political and fiscal commentator. At the age of 28 he was inducted into King Louis XV's secret spy network, Secret du Roi, going on to become the French ambassador to Russia and reportedly negotiating the 1763 Treaty of Paris, helping to bring an end to the Seven Years' War. However, the central reason for his contemporary fame was the fact that d'Eon seems to have lived the first half of his life as a man, and the second half as a woman. Indeed, historians continue to dispute the extent to which d'Eon affected this personal transformation for political reasons; some argue that cross-dressing helped to further his espionage career, whilst others emphasise d'Eon's status as a transgender icon – an individual who disrupted traditional notions of gender identity.[13]

---

13 For more about d'Eon's life, see Anna Clark, 'The Chevalier D'Eon and Wilkes: Masculinity and Politics in the Eighteenth Century', *Eighteenth-Century Studies* 32(1) (Autumn 1998): 19–48. See also Simon Burrows, Jonathan Conlin, Russell Goulbourne, Valeria Mainz (eds), *The Chevalier d'Eon and his Worlds: Gender, Espionage and Politics in the Eighteenth Century* (London: Continuum, 2010).

WHAT DOES THE STORY OF THE CHEVALIER D'EON TELL US ABOUT IDEAS OF GENDER IN THE EIGHTEENTH CENTURY? (SIGNIFICANCE)

Although this enquiry focuses on interpretations of d'Eon from his own time, there is real scope for exploring modern historians' contrasting views of d'Eon within an alternative enquiry. For this enquiry's main activity, pupils can complete a Venn-diagram card sort as they read and organise extracts from contemporary writings about d'Eon. Pupils are tasked with making inferences from these writings about the manner in which contemporaries responded to d'Eon's traversal of male and female identities; were d'Eon's contemporaries *fascinated* with d'Eon, *impressed* by his character and activities or *suspicious/wary* of his rather unique identity? Were they perhaps both fascinated and suspicious – or, indeed, did their writings veer between all three responses?

Close analysis of the accounts makes for interesting reading; the extent to which contemporaries were fascinated, impressed or suspicious of d'Eon probably tells us plenty about the individuals themselves. Radical clergyman John Horne Tooke – who met d'Eon at a dinner party in 1792 – reported to have found himself 'in the most extraordinary situation in which man ever was placed'. He was seemingly both impressed and somewhat repulsed to be sat alongside 'a lady, who has been employed in public situations at different courts, who had high rank in the army ... who has fought several duels ... who for fifty years past, all Europe has recognised in the character and dress of a gentleman.' Italian courtier Signor Collegiale de Trino proclaimed d'Eon 'a miracle', whilst Scottish writer James Boswell likened him to 'a monster'. Perhaps an anonymous English journalist most eloquently captured the confusion inherent to contemporaries' responses: 'Never before had I beheld a woman whose manners were so absurd, so masculine and so unsuitable to her sex. Always in motion, full of grimace, awkward in the habit, and impatient of the conversation of women.'[14] Using a Venn diagram works well as a tool for organising the extracts, as it helps pupils to recognise that d'Eon's contemporaries could respond in seemingly contradictory ways.

---

14 Gary Kates, 'The Transgendered World of the Chevalier/Chevalière d'Eon', *The Journal of Modern History* 67(3) (September 1995): 558–594 at 559–561.

Next, pupils are asked to consider why such reactions might have arisen. Pupils are given grids containing snippets of contextual information which, taken together, go some way towards explaining the responses exhibited by d'Eon's contemporaries. Pupils must colour-code these grids according to which of the three reactions explored in the earlier activity (*fascinated, impressed* or *suspicious*) each snippet of information most helps to explain. Having completed this activity, pupils might argue, for example, that the more wary reactions exhibited by some of d'Eon's contemporaries can be attributed to uncertainty surrounding female empowerment engendered in the pre-Revolutionary period. Others might have recognised in d'Eon a penchant for playful masquerade. Ultimately, the responses to d'Eon speak of a society that was struggling to grapple with an unprecedented degree of change and uncertainty, and the gender identity to which d'Eon aligned himself proved at once baffling and intriguing.

There are a number of conclusions that might be drawn from d'Eon's story, some of which are more uplifting than others. Pupils might infer, for example, that the predominance accorded to discussions of gender amongst contemporaries underlines d'Eon's singularity; d'Eon was the subject of intense scrutiny (and sometimes vitriol) because he was one of the first to step outside of prescribed gender norms. An alternative explanation might be that d'Eon took important steps towards the inauguration of a new gender identity and, as such, d'Eon ought to be remembered as a progenitor of the modern transgender movement. It is important, however, that pupils come away from the enquiry with an enhanced appreciation of the richness of eighteenth-century history, and an awareness that contemporaries were grappling with some of the issues that continue to exercise society today.

KEY POINTS

- Born Charles de Beaumont, the Chevalier d'Eon lived the second half of his life as a woman.

- D'Eon worked as a spy for the French king.

- Contemporaries' responses to d'Eon can be analysed as a means of exploring attitudes towards gender in the eighteenth century.

- D'Eon is remembered as a pioneering figure in the development of the transgender movement.

THE 'ATTITUDES' OF EMMA HAMILTON

- **Suggested enquiry:** Why were Grand Tourists so entranced by Emma Hamilton's 'Attitudes'? (Causation)

- **Alternative enquiry:** How did ordinary people encounter the classical world in the eighteenth century? (Similarity and difference/Evidential understanding)

In 1787, the German writer Johann Wolfgang von Goethe visited Naples and witnessed a performance of Emma Hamilton's 'Attitudes': Hamilton – the wife of British diplomat William Hamilton – assumed various poses, imitating ancient statues or characters whilst audiences attempted to guess their origins. Goethe pronounced Hamilton the perfect statue, noting 'She looses her hair, takes a pair of shawls, and makes such an alteration of stance, gesture, and countenance, that one finally thinks one is dreaming.'[15]

As a performer of motionless poses inspired by ancient statues and characters, Emma Hamilton was the originator of an art form that enjoyed enduring popularity – the buskers who today pose in stiffened metallic clothing in imitation of frozen statues are working within a tradition that dates back to Hamilton's Neapolitan drawing room. Hamilton's replication of ancient figures reflected a broader eighteenth- and nineteenth-century engagement (perhaps obsession) with the classical past, as contemporaries sought historical inspiration to steer them through the challenges of their own times.[16] Indeed, though the subject matter of 'Attitudes' may feel remote today, with ancient Greece occupying a less important role in our historical consciousness, the genre's appeal to human senses and emotion remains relatable. Pupils can appreciate the appeal of the genre – both for its edge-of-the-seat tension as the performer strives to remain immobile, and for its

---

15 Andrei Pop, 'Sympathetic Spectators: Henry Fuseli's Nightmare and Emma Hamilton's Attitudes', *Art History* 34(5) (November 2011): 934–957 at 940–941.
16 See Kate Williams, *England's Mistress: The Infamous Life of Emma Hamilton* (London: Arrow, 2007). Williams' book provides a useful overview of Hamilton's life.

imitation of emotions and experiences that are as relevant to us today as they were to the ancients who first captured them in marble.

WHY WERE GRAND TOURISTS SO ENTRANCED BY EMMA HAMILTON'S 'ATTITUDES'? (CAUSATION)

An immersion activity helps to highlight the centrality of emotion to the 'Attitudes' genre. In such an activity, pupils either listen to or participate in the retelling of one of the ancient stories from which Hamilton's performances sought inspiration. The story of Medea (a Euripidean tragedy from around 431BC) works well here. In the play, Medea was driven mad by anger at her unfaithful husband Jason; Medea schemed to poison Jason's new wife, but ultimately decided that such punishment was insufficient – so she brutally murdered her and Jason's own children. Below is an extract from an immersion activity that I created with reference to Euripides' telling of Medea's story. This helps to develop pupils' appreciation of the high drama that characterised the ancient Greek tragedies, as they begin to work out why Hamilton's 'Attitudes' attracted such interest in the late-eighteenth century.

You find yourself in the ancient city of Corinth, not far from Athens in Greece. It is a warm evening and you have come outside for a walk. You notice an odd interaction between a woman and two young children and you perch on a rock, hidden partly by an olive tree, as you watch events unfold.

The woman is dragging two small, skinny-looking boys behind her, but the boys are struggling, resisting. Their feet are dragging; perhaps they have been interrupted in sleep and are unsure of their mother's intentions.

Suddenly the woman comes to a stop and releases the children. One of the boys utters a whimper. You see a flash of something bright silver as the woman pulls an object from beneath her shawl. You squint to see what it is and a rumbling of fear begins to develop in your own stomach.

There is a moment of stillness, as though the world is holding its breath. Then, you see the woman's chest rise ... and fall ... slowly, slowly. Before you have a chance to move, the glint of silver is raised swiftly above the woman's head and then brought down in a sharp, earth-shattering motion. The stomach-curdling screams of two terrified boys ring out and suddenly it is too late … .

Next, pupils might attempt to perform some of Hamilton's 'Attitudes' for themselves, working out – using information about some of the best-known ancient figures – which characters their partners are trying to imitate. This activity requires pupils to think carefully about the way that the face and body are used to convey emotion. Photographing pupils' attempted 'Attitudes' and asking them to reflect on the success of their characterisations can help to underline Hamilton's unique mastery of the genre!

It is important that pupils are given the chance to situate Hamilton's performances within a wider eighteenth-century engagement with the classical past. Therefore, pupils explore other ancient encounters, such as visits to the newly uncovered sites of Pompeii and Herculaneum and the viewing of ancient Greek plays in popular British theatres and music halls. Finally, pupils need to understand the context for such obsessive recourse to the past, and so they examine various social and political developments that served to disturb and destabilise contemporary society. This activity helps pupils to grasp the close relationship between moments of panic and uncertainty, and attempts to find insight, inspiration or retreat in the ancient past.

By positioning Hamilton's 'Attitudes' at the centre of an enquiry, pupils are encouraged to reflect on the manner in which history can shape the present – increasingly important as we empower pupils to challenge deliberate misinterpretations of the past today. Pupils encounter, too, a woman who sought (in spite of the conventions of her time) to define herself not simply as a wife or mistress, but as a creative, skilful individual. Hamilton's 'Attitudes' are a historical peculiarity worthy of resurrection.

KEY POINTS

- Emma Hamilton, the wife of ambassador William Hamilton, performed 'Attitudes' for audiences gathered at the Hamiltons' diplomatic residence in Naples.

- Emma Hamilton responded to the contemporary fascination with the classical past, imitating ancient and mythological character in motionless scenes.

- The enquiry exemplifies the extent to which the past can be used (and abused) to shape ideas and attitudes in the present.

THE CLASSICAL ECCENTRICITIES OF RICHARD COCKLE LUCAS

- **Suggested enquiry:** What does Richard Cockle Lucas' work tell us about art and artistic taste in the nineteenth century? (Significance/Change and continuity)

- **Alternative enquiry:** Does Richard Cockle Lucas' reputation deserve to be restored? (Significance)

The nineteenth-century artist, sculptor and photographer Richard Cockle Lucas is remembered by many for his unconventionality. A quick online search throws up multiple references to this character trait: a website dedicated to Lucas' memory introduces Lucas as an 'intriguing creative figure' and a blog written on behalf of the University of Southampton's Special Collections archive refers to Lucas as a 'talented artist and engaging eccentric'.[17] The sense that Lucas worked outside of established artistic traditions is supported by a glance through some of his self-portraits. Lucas posed for photographs (intended as cartes de visites – small cards which were traded by businessmen and collectors in the nineteenth century) in such characters as the Hopeful Lover, the Impudent Man, the Modern Don, the Dark Conspirator and the Soothsayer, using physical expression and a dizzying array of props to further his characterisations. His Necromancer is particularly amusing to the modern eye: Lucas has cobbled together an assortment of rags and old cloths, and stands with his staff (an old stick) in front of a gnarly tree, staring into the distance in what he presumably hoped was an expression of wistfulness. It is particularly pleasing to imagine the preparation that must have gone into the production of such an image, as Lucas gathered his props to pose as a shabbily dressed sorcerer in front of a wizened old tree, no doubt attracting the stares of passers-by (especially as photographs took several minutes to expose in the

---

17 See http://www.richardcocklelucas.org.uk; University of Southampton Special Collections, 'Richard Cockle Lucas 1800–1883: Talented Artist and Engaging Eccentric', (6 September 2017). Available at: https://specialcollectionsuniversityofsouthampton.wordpress.com/2017/09/06/richard-cockle-lucas-1800-1883-talented-artist-and-engaging-eccentric/.

mid-nineteenth century). The fact that Lucas took to riding around Southampton in a Roman chariot – and, indeed, was widely known to believe in fairies – only added to his reputation for eccentricity.

I first came across Lucas when researching some of the manifestations of the classical obsession that gripped society in the second half of the nineteenth century. Like many of his contemporaries, Lucas was fascinated by ancient Greek art and culture; he modelled his own sculptural style on that of the ancients, and he made two large wax models of the Elgin Marbles (the Greek sculptures transported from Athens to Britain for display at the British Museum in the early nineteenth century). Lucas even designed and built a house known as the Tower of the Winds in Surrey, inspired by the octagonal marble clocktower that had been built by the ancient Greeks in Athens. The unique manner in which Lucas expressed his admiration for the ancient world was not incidental to his story; indeed, it reflects the extent to which classical art and culture was considered fit for appropriation, malleable to the concerns and demands of the contemporary world.

In a society that places great stock in conformity and compliance, exposing pupils to eccentrics like Richard Cockle Lucas can only be a good thing. It is not simply a case of offering role models for young people (although I would have great respect for any teenager who chooses to model him or herself upon Lucas!). Building enquiries around individuals who transgressed social and cultural norms helps to validate pupils' own idiosyncrasies, encouraging them to express themselves more freely.

WHAT DOES RICHARD COCKLE LUCAS' WORK TELL US ABOUT ART AND ARTISTIC TASTE IN THE NINETEENTH CENTURY? (SIGNIFICANCE/ CHANGE AND CONTINUITY)

Lucas' story can be woven into this enquiry as pupils examine the various trends and movements from which Lucas drew inspiration – or to which he contributed his own ideas and designs. Study of artistic works (like, in this case, Lucas' sculptures, photographs and cartes de visites) helps to develop pupils' source analysis skills, as well as being an important end in itself as we try to equip pupils with the language and tools with which to comprehend a range of cultural products.

The enquiry therefore centres upon close study of Lucas' works. Pupils are guided through an analysis of these artworks in stages: they make initial inferences based on their examination of the images; next, they add annotations based on additional contextual information they have been given; and finally, they jot down any questions that they still have with regard to Lucas or his artworks. This final activity is important; pupils ought to be encouraged to recognise that history does not always provide all the answers, and that it is acceptable – even to be encouraged – that we continue to pose questions of the historical material.

Everyone knows a Richard Cockle Lucas: he is the man or woman that does not quite fit, and in whose company we feel a slight sense of disequilibrium because we are not entirely certain how we ought to respond to their views, appearance or mannerisms. Yet Lucas' obsession with classical history was not in itself unusual. Many of his contemporaries felt a similar connection with the ancient Greeks (though admittedly Lucas' methods of expressing this connection were rather extreme). Placing Lucas' passion within the context of its time therefore helps us make sense of an individual who eschewed the norms of accepted social behaviour. It also helps us to convey some of the ways in which an appreciation of the past can figure in contemporary society, as individuals seek historic parallels or models through which to make sense of their own ideas and experiences in the present day.

KEY POINTS

- Richard Cockle Lucas was a nineteenth-century artist, sculptor and photographer. He was known locally to be something of an eccentric.

- Lucas was obsessed with the classical past, and often drew inspiration for his work from ancient Greek figures or architecture.

- Art historical analysis helps to build pupils' source analysis skills.

- Studying *eccentrics* like Lucas validates pupils' own idiosyncrasies.

THE ORIGINAL ARTFUL DODGER: RENTON NICHOLSON

> - **Suggested enquiry:** Was E. P. Thompson right about the making of the English working class? (Interpretations)
>
> - **Alternative enquiry:** What can we learn from Renton Nicholson about working-class life in the nineteenth century? (Evidential understanding)

In his 1860 autobiography, the entrepreneur, entertainment impresario and man-about-town Renton Nicholson addressed his readers:

'Let me shake hands with you at starting, for we are bound to travel together in sunlight and in shade, in lively day and dismal night-time; through narrow, devious passages and broad ways; in the cells of poverty, and the mansions of wealth; through cities, towns and hamlets, where humanity dwells amid innocence and corruption, where base metal contrasts with unalloyed gold.'[18]

This address captures the contrast which characterised Nicholson's own life and career, as he veered between success and failure, respectability and misconduct, polite society and the shady underworld. It also reflects the complex and very human nature of Nicholson's story – a story that serves to complicate ideas about the lives of working men and women in the nineteenth century.

Nicholson was an interesting character and his self-reflections often feel contradictory: at times he wrote nostalgically about his formative experiences, whilst at others he displayed an unattractive talent for profiting at the expense of others. Pupils will find some evidence that Nicholson acted as a champion of the working class; he was generous in promoting the interests of his fellow Londoners and supported various working-class initiatives. He certainly contributed, in his own

---

18 Renton Nicholson, *The Lord Chief Baron Nicholson: An Autobiography* (London: George Vickers, 1855), pp. 1–2.

way, to establishing a set of working-class traditions in London's East End, as he presided over sittings of the popular Judge and Jury Society (in which Nicholson oversaw mock trials based on celebrated court cases of the day). However, the extent to which Nicholson can be seen as a true working-class hero is called into question through his exploitation of women and, ultimately, through his pursuit of personal wealth; Nicholson was known for putting on *illustrated lectures* in which the impresario gave talks on the benefits of classical art – with scantily clad women appearing on the stage behind him. Social reformers of the time were not fooled by Nicholson's pretensions to culture, likening the performances to public prostitution. The *working class* is a problematic concept, but it is one that pupils ought to be encouraged to explore at Key Stage 3 – especially because the lexicon of class remains ubiquitous in contemporary society. If pupils are to explore the notion of class from an historical point of view, then E. P. Thompson's *The Making of the English Working Class* (1963) seems to offer a good starting point. This enquiry is framed, therefore, around Thompson's study. It challenges pupils to engage with the arguments put forward in this groundbreaking work of historiography – and, perhaps, to pick some of them apart, using Renton Nicholson's story as a means of doing this in a convincing and evidence-based manner.

WAS E. P. THOMPSON RIGHT ABOUT THE MAKING OF THE ENGLISH WORKING CLASS? (INTERPRETATIONS)

Pupils begin by engaging with extracts from Thompson's book (the Preface provides a useful starting point to locate these).[19] They delve into some of the arguments Thompson made about the working-class 'consciousness' that supposedly developed in the course of the nineteenth century, as well as the aspirations and ambitions that these labourers harboured in spite of the depersonalising impact of the Industrial Revolution. Having developed a basic understanding of where Thompson's arguments departed so significantly from historians who came

---

19 E. P. Thompson, *The Making of the English Working Class* (London: Penguin, 1991). Alternatively, extracts from the book can be found online. Pupils should read Thompson's claims about the development of a working-class 'consciousness'. Thompson claimed that a sense of 'community' increasingly separated 'the poor stockinger, the Luddite cropper, the "obsolete" handloom weaver, the "utopian" artisan' from their middle and upper-class superiors (p. 12).

before him, pupils are asked to consider how, exactly, we might go about assessing the accuracy of Thompson's claims; what would we be looking for as evidence of a working-class consciousness in a man or woman that lived in the nineteenth century?[20]

This is an important stage in the enquiry; by proposing suggestions in this manner, pupils are essentially coming up with the criteria they will use to analyse the evidence, framing an enquiry which challenges the validity of an historical interpretation. Pupils' suggestions can be refined and streamlined into three key themes, and these transferred to a recording grid. Pupils must then identify evidence from sources relating to the life and career of Renton Nicholson, to indicate ways in which Nicholson fulfilled – or did not fulfil – the criteria for Thompson's working-class consciousness.

Nicholson offers a useful case study in nineteenth-century working-class culture and pupils will be well equipped to judge the extent to which Nicholson fulfilled Thompson's claims for a working-class consciousness, having studied sources relating to Nicholson's life in the East End. Once they have examined Nicholson's career, pupils can end the enquiry by writing letters to E. P. Thompson, outlining the extent to which his claims can be validated with reference to the evidence.

In studying the history of the working class, it is important that pupils develop a more nuanced picture of the men and women who purportedly characterised this section of society. This will empower them to critique some of the reductionist assumptions that have been made by historians in the past, and to move beyond problematic stereotypes that have been handed down to them by popular books and films. Renton Nicholson's story corrects a number of popular misconceptions about the Victorian working class: namely, that nineteenth-century orphans were always impoverished and helpless, that belonging to a labouring class dictated a kind of kinsmanship and loyalty to be displayed to one's fellows, and that the poorly educated were destined for lives of misery and degradation. Nicholson was not a straightforward hero, but nor was he a genuine villain; it is perhaps for this reason that he is particularly worthy of historical study.

KEY POINTS

● Entrepreneur Renton Nicholson emerged as a working-class success story in the nineteenth century.

---

20 E. P. Thompson, *The Making of the English Working Class*, p. 9.

- Nicholson established a number of working-class traditions in London's East End, including mock trials that saw Nicholson preside over re-enactments of celebrated court cases.

- Pupils can use Nicholson's story to determine the extent to which E. P. Thompson's claims of a working-class consciousness had really developed in the nineteenth century.

CHARLES KINGSLEY, THE VICTORIAN POLYMATH

- **Suggested enquiry:** What did Charles Kingsley's ideas and beliefs suggest about religion in Victorian Britain? (Significance)

- **Alternative enquiry:** How accurately did Kingsley's *The Water-Babies* describe the lives of Victorian children? (Interpretations/Similarity and difference)

Charles Kingsley was one of the most complex, contradictory and incongruous characters of the Victorian era – and, as such, he is an individual around whom a number of interesting historical enquiries can be constructed. Born in Devon in 1819, Kingsley was no doubt inspired by his father's service as a local reverend to pursue a career in the priesthood. In 1844 Kingsley became rector of Eversley in Hampshire and fifteen years later was appointed chaplain to Queen Victoria. He also served as professor of modern history at the University of Cambridge. Kingsley's interests were varied; he advocated for the rights of the working classes when he wrote for the journal *Politics for the People*, and he promoted Muscular Christianity as a philosophical movement, according to which men were encouraged to carry out their patriotic duties whilst exhibiting the characteristics of self-sacrifice, physical masculinity and classical athleticism. Influenced to some extent by the ideas of Charles Darwin and other evolutionists, Kingsley also developed an interest in spiritualism – and the idea of nature representing a tool of divinity. Kingsley's novels reflected his passion for, variously, religion, magic, history, the plight of the working classes, public health and the issues of race and slavery.

WHAT DID CHARLES KINGSLEY'S IDEAS AND BELIEFS SUGGEST ABOUT RELIGION IN VICTORIAN BRITAIN? (SIGNIFICANCE)

An enquiry into ideas, attitudes and beliefs in the Victorian period is lent interest and relatability through the study of extracts from Kingsley's *The Water-Babies: A Fairy Tale for a Land-Baby*. Written in 1862–1863, the novel (which was first published in serialised form) told the story of Tom, a chimney sweep who embarks upon a series of lessons and adventures after having been transformed into a 'water-baby'. Much can be learnt or inferred from the novel about religious or spiritual belief, ideas of evolution and scientific/moral progress, the experiences of the working classes and attitudes towards childhood during the mid-Victorian period. The passages about Tom's life as a chimney sweep are particularly eye-catching ('He cried when he had to climb the dark flues, rubbing his poor knees and elbows raw ... and when his master beat him, which he did every day in the week; and when he had not enough to eat, which happened every day in the week likewise'),[21] although more profound insight might be gleaned from the novel's reflections on the nature of belief/disbelief and proof ('"But there are no such things as water-babies." How do you know that? Have you been there to see? And if you had been there to see, and had seen none, that would not prove that there was none.').[22] Kingsley also used the novel to conceal comments (which are extremely troubling to modern audiences) about the nature of human evolution; a group of humans referred to as the 'Doasyoulikes' are left to 'do as they like', and eventually degenerate to become gorillas, with Tom noting that they are growing 'no better than savages'.[23]

The enquiry might therefore see pupils make inferences from extracts taken from *The Water-Babies*, before cross-referencing their inferences with additional contextual information about the nature of religious, political and scientific belief in the Victorian period.[24] It is useful to spend time unpicking some of the assumptions

---

21 Charles Kingsley, *The Water-Babies: A Fairy Tale for a Land-Baby* [eBook] (Urbana, IL: Project Gutenberg, 2008), p. 1. Available at: https://www.gutenberg.org/files/25564/25564-h/25564-h.htm.
22 Kingsley, *The Water-Babies*, p. 54.
23 Kingsley, *The Water-Babies*, pp. 189–190.
24 Richard J. Helmstadter and Bernard Lightman (eds), *Victorian Faith in Crisis: Essays on Continuity and Chance in Nineteenth-Century Religious Belief* (Stanford: Stanford University Press, 1990). This book provides a useful overview of changing religious beliefs in the Victorian period.

and stereotypes featured in the book (relating to less evolved human groups or races, as well as to Jewish people, Catholics and the Irish); only by doing so will pupils approach an understanding of why these assumptions are so problematic. Pupils can then reach their conclusions about the extent to which Kingsley's novel can be considered to offer useful insight into the nature of beliefs and attitudes in the Victorian period.

A creative and engaging way to finish the enquiry is to challenge pupils to create their own ethical tracts for the modern day. Kingsley's work has overtly moralising overtones, with characters assigned names like 'Mrs Doasyouwouldbedoneby' and the 'Doasyoulikes'. Ask pupils to consider the messages they believe contemporary writers or politicians might wish to convey, and challenge them to come up with their own character names to reflect these. It would be an interesting exercise to ask them to think of different names according to the individual, group or party concerned – and, finally, to create names reflecting their own views.

KEY POINTS

- Charles Kingsley was a polymath, with interests ranging from religion and magic to public health, race and slavery.

- Kingsley's *The Water-Babies* offers insight into contemporary ideas and attitudes.

- Using extracts from novels and books is an engaging way of exploring past societies.

- Lingering on unsavoury or problematic stereotypes present in books like *The Water-Babies* is important if we are to challenge these ideas.

THE FEMALE PRIORITY OF EXISTENCE: ROSA FRANCES SWINEY

- **Suggested enquiry:** How did the feminist movement evolve in the nineteenth and twentieth centuries? (Change and continuity)

- **Alternative enquiry:** What impact did Rosa Frances Swiney have on the suffrage movement? (Significance/Consequence)

Life, argued Rosa Frances Swiney in 1909, was feminine, as 'all emanations are from that mystery of the Divine Mother... Even as science reveals that all life has a feminine origin ... The Feminine is therefore the inner nature of man, and woman as the most highly evolved organism ... is the objective representative of the Divine Feminine.' Contrary to the views expressed by conventional religions, philosophies and theories, the idea that the male was secondary to the female – and therefore of little importance (biologically) in comparison with the female[25] – was the basis for Swiney's highly controversial feminist vision. Swiney's contribution to the early twentieth-century feminist movement was to argue that women were entitled to political, sexual and social rights on the grounds of the significant contribution they made to the 'development and advancement of the English Race'.[26]

Born in India in 1847 (her father was a member of the Dragoon Guards assigned to safeguard the East India Company's interests abroad), Swiney took a keen interest in the British imperial project from an early age. She married John Swiney, major of the Madras Staff Corps, and although she and her husband lived initially in India, Swiney moved to England with three of her children in 1877. It was after 1890 that she began to play a more active role in local politics, and in 1890 she

25 Jessica Albrecht, 'Agency and Impact of a Theosophical Feminist in the Imperial Discourse on Motherhood and Race', *Academia* (2018), p. 1. Available at: https://www.academia.edu/38559189/Mrs._Rosa_Frances_Swiney_Agency_and_Impact_of_a_Theosophical_Feminist_in_the_Imperial_Discourse_on_Motherhood_and_Race.
26 Albrecht, 'Agency and Impact', p. 11.

co-founded the Cheltenham Women's Suffrage Society. She was also a member of the National Woman's Social and Political Union – a militant suffrage organisation that would become famous for the dramatic activities of Emmeline Pankhurst, Christabel Pankhurst and others in the years after 1910. Swiney's political convictions had imperial undercurrents. She argued that if the Empire was to be sustained, women's contributions (in terms of their labour, as well as their roles as mothers) needed to be recognised; the most productive society was one in which men and women worked together to raise their children, furthering the causes of purity and sexual morality. Swiney criticised the ways in which Indian women were treated by their own husbands and families, as well as by British men. For her, this was symbolic of the 'degeneration' of the Indian 'race'; in times of past glory ancient Indian society had revered women and respected their natural rights.[27] Swiney was also a eugenicist in the sense that she believed, ultimately, that human evolution would reach its highest phase once the human species became fully feminised.

Swiney's story deserves its place within an enquiry on the British suffrage movement, as her beliefs and arguments lend nuance to our understanding of the campaign's evolution. Delivering lessons on any topic (but particularly the suffrage movement) on an annual basis can desensitise us a little to the material we deliver – but pupils' horrified and awe-filled responses always serve to remind me of just how inspirational the suffrage campaigners were. Emily Davison's story is a real crowd-pleaser; pupils can scarcely believe how bravely Davison endured the brutal force-feeding campaigns instigated by the government, and they are shocked when they are presented with evidence of Davison's intentional martyrdom at Derby Day. The suffrage campaigners were indeed heroes of the feminist movement. As with any topic, though, it is important to add nuance where we can. Swiney's story – and, in particular, her rather controversial racial politics – helps us to do this.

27 Albrecht, 'Agency and Impact', p. 16.

HOW DID THE FEMINIST MOVEMENT EVOLVE IN THE NINETEENTH AND TWENTIETH CENTURIES? (CHANGE AND CONTINUITY)

Swiney's ideas are well situated within a change and continuity enquiry on the suffrage movement, during which pupils examine the changing nature of the tactics used by the campaigners. A card sort works well here, allowing pupils to first organise information into chronological order (with the x-axis of their graph running from earliest to latest), before deciding how militant or violent the activities were (y-axis). Pupils' understanding of the changing landscape in which these tactics emerged can be fostered with the distribution of context cards; based on these, pupils can be encouraged to verbalise links between the suffragettes' activities and the changing political climate (such as the Third Reform Bill of 1884 – which saw an amendment to include women be rejected – and the defeat of the proposed amendment to the Reform Bill in 1913).

Swiney's controversial views cannot, of course, be excused – but they can be placed in their proper context, and examining the impact of social and political developments in Swiney's lifetime helps to do this. Finally, it is useful to give pupils the chance to engage with the debate on the extent to which suffrage campaigners ought to be considered terrorists. Many pupils will have interesting views on whether or not this emotive label applies to the feminists of the early twentieth century, and an interesting (and, crucially, well-informed) debate is likely to follow.

KEY POINTS

- Rosa Frances Swiney was a feminist and suffrage campaigner who argued that female equality was justified on imperial grounds.

- She argued that women deserved the vote, given their important role in the 'advancement of the English Race'.

- Swiney's story adds nuance to pupils' understanding of the suffrage movement in Britain and beyond.

- It is important that pupils appreciate the changing nature of the suffragists' tactics over time.

'COME ALONG AND BE ONE OF THE BOYS': VESTA TILLEY

- **Suggested enquiry:** What can the music hall tell us about women in Victorian and Edwardian society? (Significance)

- **Alternative enquiry:** How did Vesta Tilley challenge the traditional 'angel in the house' stereotype? (Similarity and difference)

In one of her most famous music hall songs, Vesta Tilley implored her audience to 'Come, come, come, and be one of the midnight sons / Come along and be one of the boys / And join the throng and sing this song / And be one of the boys, be one of the boys.'[28] Tilley certainly heeded her own advice; during her lengthy music hall career – at one point where she was England's highest-earning woman – Tilley worked as a male impersonator, delivering patriotic songs dressed in combat uniform as she tried to promote enlistment to the army.

Tilley (whose real name was Matilda Alice Powles) was born in 1864, one of Matilda and Henry Powles' thirteen children. Tilley's father was a musician and he encouraged her onto the stage; she was performing in public from the age of 3. Tilley became known for impersonating famous male characters (including the then-famous opera singer Sims Reeves) and later in her career she performed male roles exclusively, claiming that 'I felt that I could express myself better if I were dressed as a boy.'[29] Tilley's fame coincided with – and was promoted by – the explosion in popularity of the music hall. By the 1880s, the music hall was a ubiquitous form of popular entertainment with London-based halls like the Canterbury, the Alhambra, the Empire and the Palace Theatre enjoying the patronage of visitors from all classes. Tilley's character, Burlington Bertie, was particularly well known and she toured British and American theatres, as well as recording songs (she was one of the first to do so in England) and appearing in pantomimes. When war broke

---

28 Vesta Tilley, 'Come and Be One of the Midnight Sons' [song], written by Worton David and Kenneth Lyle (1897). Lyrics available at: https://monologues.co.uk/musichall/Songs-C/Come-And-Be-Midnight-Sons.htm.
29 Anthony Slide, *The Encyclopedia of Vaudeville* (Jackson, MS: University Press of Mississippi, 2012), p. 502.

out in 1914, Tilley supported the recruitment drive by performing songs including 'Your King and Country Want You' and 'The Army of Today's All Right'. Some of her songs did carry a rather less optimistic note; in 'A Bit of a Blighty One', she sang about a soldier whose wounds gave him the chance to return to England.[30] Tilley retired in 1920 and lived in Monte Carlo until her death in 1952.

WHAT CAN THE MUSIC HALL TELL US ABOUT WOMEN IN VICTORIAN AND EDWARDIAN SOCIETY? (SIGNIFICANCE)

I teach this enquiry within a broader scheme of work on Victorian and Edwardian society, and it is the most unashamedly social interlude in my entire Key Stage 3 curriculum. It is also one of the most popular amongst the pupils I teach – proving (at least to me) that Year 9 pupils neither want nor need their history diet to be composed exclusively of bloody battles and even bloodier revolutions.

In the enquiry, pupils are first presented with a series of paintings depicting the idealised Victorian or Edwardian woman; these include Alexander Rossi's *On the Shores of Bognor Regis* (1887), Dante Gabriel Rossetti's *The Girlhood of Mary Virgin* (1848) and Marcus Stone's *Lost in Thought* (1879).[31] Pupils are asked to propose adjectives that describe the women in these portraits – they tend to come up with words like 'respectable', 'devout' and 'innocent'. The enquiry is then set up and the music hall figures – whose appearance, manner and characteristics contrast strongly with notions of the ideal Victorian or Edwardian woman – can be introduced.

In her article, '"The Woman of To-day": The Fin de Siècle Women of The Music Hall and Theatre Review', historian Patricia O'Hara argued that the singing and dancing women of the music hall posed a threat to conservative Victorian ideas about

---

30 Vesta Tilley, 'Your King and Country Want You' [song], written by Paul Rubens (1914); 'The Army of Today's All Right' [song], written by Fred W. Leigh and Kenneth Lyle (1914); 'A Bit of a Blighty One' [song], written by Herman Darewski and Arthur Wimperis (1918).
31 For Rossi's painting, see https://fineartamerica.com/featured/on-the-shores-of-bognor-regis-alexander-m-rossi.html. For Rossetti's painting, see https://www.tate.org.uk/art/artworks/rossetti-the-girlhood-of-mary-virgin-n04872. For Marcus Stone's painting, see https://www.myartprints.co.uk/a/stone-marcus/lost-in-thought-2.html.

gender.[32] Pupils are challenged to substantiate or challenge this interpretation with evidence, and they plot a series of case studies onto a continuum to determine the extent to which the individuals in question posed a threat/challenge to contemporary notions of female respectability and conservatism, which were encapsulated by the image of the 'angel in the house' (a phrase popularised by a poem, published between 1854 and 1862, by Coventry Padmore).[33] The case studies include Vesta Tilley, Marie Loftus, Bessie Bonehill and the acrobatic performer known as Zaeo – all of whom served in different ways to defy convention (through scanty dress, the *indecent* exposure of legs, ankles and armpits and *impertinent* male personification). Finally, pupils decide how far they agree with O'Hara's interpretation, outlining their conclusions in a paragraph.

Popular entertainment is one of the best lenses through which to explore ideas, attitudes and interests in the late nineteenth and early twentieth centuries. It both reflected and helped to curate ordinary people's views and, as such, a study of music hall and variety theatre can offer real insight into popular tastes (in music, dance and fashion), social concerns and priorities of the day, and even the political convictions of working-class men and women.

Vesta Tilley and her colleagues stood at the vanguard of a dynamic movement for social transformation. These performers opened the eyes of society to the possibility of new roles and opportunities for women; they *performed* social and political change, providing concrete models and examples from which ordinary women could draw inspiration. As such, Tilley's story adds important nuance to the history of the feminist movement in Britain as it helps pupils to recognise the role that was (quite literally) played by transgressive women in helping to promote calls for female equality and enfranchisement at the beginning of the twentieth century.

KEY POINTS

● Born Matilda Alice Powles, Vesta Tilley was one of the best-known and highest-paid music hall performers of the early twentieth century.

---

32 Patricia O'Hara, '"The Woman of To-day": The Fin de Siècle Women of The Music Hall and Theatre Review', *Victorian Periodicals Review*, 30(2) (1997): 141–156 at 143. See also Dagmar Kift, *The Victorian Music Hall: Culture, Class and Conflict* (Cambridge: Cambridge University Press, 1996). This book is a classic study of the Victorian music hall.

33 For more about this Victorian stereotype, see Anne Hogan and Andrew Bradstock (eds), *Women of Faith in Victorian Culture: Reassessing the Angel in the House* (Basingstoke: Macmillan, 1998).

- Tilley was a male impersonator and she claimed that she was able to better express herself 'dressed as a boy'.

- Tilley's performances can be situated within the context of the feminist movement, as early twentieth-century feminists took it upon themselves to subvert traditional notions of femininity.

CONCLUSION: PLANNING FOR A DIVERSE CURRICULUM

In my experience, history teachers are very good at collecting stories and anecdotes from the past. We read books, listen to podcasts, visit museums, scroll through Twitter and sometimes even interview our own relatives – and then we stockpile these stories, reminding ourselves to do something with them at some point in the future. My school planner is littered with scribbled references to individuals I have come across in textbooks, and I have stored a number of notes in my phone to jog my memory about case studies I am intending to weave into lessons or schemes of work in the future. The problem, of course, is that these stories are easily forgotten and our busy schedules prevent us from making the most of opportunities for building meaningful enquiries around them. Whilst name-dropping the odd interesting individual mid-lesson can make for an engaging interlude, the character and shape of the curriculum is not fundamentally improved if, for example, we simply state that Elizabeth Alkin was there when the English Civil War was going on, or that Indian soldiers took part in the fighting during World War One.

I hope that the enquiries outlined in this book might be used to enrich the delivery of well-established themes and topics at Key Stages 3, 4 and 5 in particular. Now I would like to outline some suggestions for teachers wishing to develop the diversifying project for themselves – and to suggest practical ways in which we might move away from a tokenistic, anecdotal approach, towards one which is genuinely reflective of the diversity and richness of the past.

Here are some starting points that teachers might wish to adopt or adapt:

- It seems a rather trivial suggestion, but invest in a notebook that can be dedicated to ideas and case studies you intend to weave into your planning. There are several advantages to using a paper notebook instead of an electronic one. First, a paper notebook cannot be lost in the case of technological failure; and second, an A4 or A5 notebook allows you to devote entire physical pages to discrete case studies/enquiries.

● In my notebook, I like to organise the pages using a Cornell notes-style template. The Cornell notes approach – first developed by Cornell University education professor Walter Pauk in the 1950s – is based on the idea that information is best retained when it is carefully organised.[1] I divide each of my pages into a large *Notes* section (where I jot down the basic information about the story or case study I have come across, along with any additional research); a smaller *Lesson* section (where I begin to plan how the story or case study might be translated into – or linked with – an activity, lesson or scheme of work); and a final *Summary* section (in which I write one or two sentences reminding myself why the story deserves to be told, or what it has to tell pupils about a particular topic or theme). Taken as a whole, this method helps me to translate abstract ideas into concrete lesson plans.

● Develop a bank of lesson activities you can draw upon when planning, in order to help pupils develop their skills in relation to each of the second-order concepts (significance, causation, consequence, change and continuity, similarity and difference, evidential understanding and interpretations). A couple of years ago, I created a resource booklet for a trainee teacher which contained three or four templates for activities that worked well in conjunction with each of these concepts. The idea was that the teacher could select the activity that seemed most appropriate for the lesson or enquiry they were planning at the time, and simply slot the material into the template. As the enquiries outlined in the main chapters of this book have demonstrated, many activities are transferable: for example, radar graphs work well as a method by which to unpack the concept of consequence, whilst the concept of change and continuity can be fruitfully explored through card sorts or timeline activities. Building up this resource bank ought to make the planning process feel less daunting.

● Adopt a flexible approach to lesson and curriculum planning and be prepared to make changes following discussion with other teachers, as well as feedback from pupils themselves. Jamie Byrom and Michael Riley have referred to this approach as 'professional wrestling': they note the process whereby history teachers grapple with such issues as content, outline and

---

1   See https://lsc.cornell.edu/how-to-study/taking-notes/cornell-note-taking-system/.

depth, and claim that 'successful teachers spend huge amounts of time and energy wrestling with lessons and learning activities.'[2] Byrom and Riley's wrestling metaphor reflects the manner according to which teachers arrive at the most effective enquiries: it is a process of careful reflection and adaptation which is scrutinised at every stage to ensure that both teacher(s) and pupils understand why they are studying the topic in question, and how the chosen lesson activities help to develop essential comprehension and skills.

- Finally, one method that I have found useful for determining the extent to which pupils' learning outcomes match my own intended outcomes for the enquiry is the use of 'takeaways' at the end of a lesson or activity. Working in much the same way as an 'exit ticket', pupils note down (or verbalise) the top three things they have learnt, before perhaps sharing these with a classmate or with me. The activity can be adapted depending on your aims for the lesson: sometimes I ask Key Stage 5 pupils to give me two content-based takeaways and one takeaway linked to the skills they have developed, or I might frame the activity along the lines of 'What three things would Claudia Jones want us to take away from this lesson?', for example, or 'What three things would [social/political/Marxist] historians tell us were most important about today's lesson?' as a way of helping pupils develop their appreciation of contrasting interpretations. The activity helps to make pupils' learning visible, underlining to the pupils themselves and to others what they have learned. It is a great way of identifying misconceptions, too.

In weaving greater diversity into our schemes of work, it is important that we as teachers feel a sense of ownership – and to do this, we should select stories and case studies that we find engaging and illuminating. Below, I have outlined a number of online resources that might represent useful starting points for further research. Of course, more detailed insight relating to the individuals and events in question can be found in academic books and articles (some of which are referenced in this book). However, initial inspiration might be sought in the following list:

---

2   Jamie Byrom and Michael Riley, 'Professional Wrestling in the History Department: A Case Study in Planning the Teaching of the British Empire at Key Stage 3', *Teaching History* 112 (2003): 6–14 at 14.

Resource	Use this resource for …
This Day in History	History.com gives short overviews of daily historical events (www.history.com/this-day-in-history) – and the archive allows you to read information relating to all 365 days of the year. In addition, public historian Dan Snow (@thehistoryguy) often tweets about important events or developments from the past, and On This Day She (@OnThisDayShe) introduces the stories of overlooked women from history, which can be used as the basis for interesting and unique enquiries.
Women's History Network	This website (www.womenshistorynetwork.org) provides information and links to resources for teachers wishing to promote women's history in the classroom. The resources are organised by theme (i.e. Black History, US history, First and Second World War), which is useful if you know the topic into which you intend to slot the enquiry.
Our Migration Story	Having started to teach the Edexcel Migrants in Britain course in 2021, I have found this website (www.ourmigrationstory.org.uk) an invaluable resource for developing my own knowledge and understanding. The website features a number of case studies from each time period: for example, a petition by Dr Hector Nunes is described as part of the wider story of African freedom and slavery in Tudor England, and the story of Sophia Duleep Singh helps to exemplify (and complicate) the history of South Asian migration to Britain in the nineteenth century.

Resource	Use this resource for ...
Centre for the Study of the Legacies of British Slavery	University College London has put together a large online database tracing the surprising reach of the compensation monies handed out after the abolition of slavery across the British Empire in 1833 (see www.ucl. ac.uk/lbs). I have used this resource as the basis for planning enquiries, and I have also encouraged pupils to familiarise themselves with the database: pupils can research family/local history, and it is possible to identify well-known individuals, businesses and estates that benefitted from this huge payout.
Institute of Historical Research: Teaching British Histories of Race, Migration and Empire	The Institute of Historical Research has gathered a number of resources to help promote the delivery of the overlooked histories of colonialism and migration (www. history.ac.uk/library/collections/teaching-british-histories-race-migration-and-empire#key-stage-3-11-14-year-olds). Organised by key stage, the website is easy to navigate and contains a variety of materials, including links to useful websites and videos, lesson plans and outlines, teaching packs and ready-made teaching resources.
African Kingdoms	During the first lockdown in 2020, history teachers Nick Dennis and Trevor Getz – along with historian Toby Green – produced a series of webinars on African kingdoms including Asante, Benin and Kongo, and the resources from these webinars (along with Toby Green's electronic textbook for teaching the African Kingdoms A Level option with the exam board OCR) are available online (www.africankingdoms.co.uk). These have helped develop my understanding of how to approach the delivery of African history in the classroom and have pointed me towards sources and case studies that I have woven into my planning.

The curation of a more diverse, representative curriculum inevitably raises a number of pedagogical (and ethical) questions. Which case studies and enquiries might be included, and which must be left out or deemphasised in order to make room for new material? Whose histories should we tell? Ought the aim of our curriculum be to inspire, surprise, reassure or simply to educate? These are questions to which the answers will depend largely on context, and each teacher's views on the nature and purpose of history education. We might decide, for example, that the pupils in our own school setting would benefit from engaging with stories relating to a particular identity (which may or may not link to the pupils' own identities). We might alternatively be dictated by certain school or department-wide priorities, such as the wish to deliver content in a certain sequence, or to interleave themes at Key Stages 3 and 4. There are various factors that will impact on the manner in which we set about diversifying our own curriculum material.

The key, as this book has sought to emphasise, is to allow the stories that we select to speak for themselves. People in the past did not exist simply to fulfil our own moralising or didactic agendas, and their experiences should not be interpolated into a fixed or predetermined narrative. The importance (and joy) of history is that it allows for multiple interpretations to exist, and the stories that we tell will resonate in different ways for all the pupils who are exposed to them. Weaving diversity into the history curriculum is one of the best ways that we can foster passion for our subject. Beyond this, the diversifying project helps to define and embed a sense of self as young people grapple with the complex, divergent and sometimes unexpected nature of identity in the past.

BIBLIOGRAPHY

Adams, Gene (1984). 'Dido Elizabeth Belle: A Black Girl at Kenwood', *Camden History Review* 12: 2. Available at: http://www.mirandakaufmann.com/uploads/1/2/2/5/12258270/dido-elizabeth-belle_-a-black-girl-at-kenwood.pdf.

Adams, John (1823). *Remarks on the Country Extending From Cape Palmas to the River Congo*. London: G and W. B. Whittaker.

Albrecht, Jessica (2018). 'Agency and Impact of a Theosophical Feminist in the Imperial Discourse on Motherhood and Race', *Academia*, p. 1. Available at: https://www.academia.edu/38559189/Mrs._Rosa_Frances_Swiney_Agency_and_Impact_of_a_Theosophical_Feminist_in_the_Imperial_Discourse_on_Motherhood_and_Race.

Anon. (1726). *An Enquiry how the Wild Youth, Lately Taken in the Woods Near Hanover*. London: H. Parker.

Bacon, Reginald H. (1897). *The City of Blood*. London: Arnold.

Bagshawe Harrison, George (1933). *Shakespeare under Elizabeth*. New York: H. Holt & Co.

Bank of England (2021). 'Choosing Banknote Characters' (22 June). Available at: https://www.bankofengland.co.uk/banknotes/banknote-characters.

Barton, Keith C. and Levstik, Linda S. (2004). *Teaching History for the Common Good*. Abingdon: Routledge.

Blankenship, Mary and Reeves, Richard V. (2020). 'From the George Floyd Moment to a Black Lives Matter Movement, in Tweets', *Brookings* (10 July). Available at: https://www.brookings.edu/blog/up-front/2020/07/10/from-the-george-floyd-moment-to-a-black-lives-matter-movement-in-tweets/.

Blincoe, Robert (1832). *A Memoir of Robert Blincoe*. Manchester: J. Doherty.

Boissoneault, Lorraine (2017). 'The Speech That Brought India to the Brink of Independence', *Smithsonian Magazine* (8 August). Available at: https://www.smithsonianmag.com/history/speech-brought-india-brink-independence-180964366/.

Bray, Alan (1982). *Homosexuality in Renaissance England*. New York: Columbia University Press.

Brady, Tim (2021). *Three Ordinary Girls*. New York: Kensington Publishing.

Brighton & Hove Black History (n.d.). 'African Kings in Brighton'. Available at: https://black-history.org.uk/project/three-african-kings-visit-brighton-in-1895/.

Brinkhurst-Cuff, Charlie (2018). *Mother Country: Real Stories of the Windrush Children*. London: Headline Publishing Group.

Bromley, Matt (2020). 'Black Lives Matter: How Schools Must Respond', *SecEd* (25 November). Available at: https://www.sec-ed.co.uk/best-practice/black-lives-matter-how-schools-must-respond-curriculum-racism-george-floyd-teaching-colston/.

Burrows, Simon, Conlin, Jonathan, Goulbourne, Russell and Mainz, Valeria (eds) (2010). *The Chevalier d'Eon and his Worlds: Gender, Espionage and Politics in the Eighteenth Century*. London: Continuum.

Butler, Josephine (1886). 'The Double Standard of Morality', *W. B. Stead Resource Site*. First published in *The Philanthropist* (October). Available at: https://www.attackingthedevil.co.uk/related/morality.php.

Byfield, Judith, Brown, Carolyn, Parsons, Timothy, Sikainga and Ahmad, Alawad (eds) (2015). *Africa and World War II*. Cambridge: Cambridge University Press.

Catlin, George (1841). *Letters and Notes on the Manners, Customs and Conditions of the North American Indians*. London: Tosswill and Myers.

Byrom, Jamie and Riley, Michael (2003). 'Professional Wrestling in the History Department: A Case Study in Planning the Teaching of the British Empire at Key Stage 3', *Teaching History* 112: 6–14.

Catlin, George (1852). *Adventures of the Ojibbeway and Iowa Indians in England, France and Belgium, Being Notes of Eight Years' Travels and Residence in Europe with his North American Indian Collection*. London: published by author.

Chambers, Anne (2018). *Grace O'Malley: The Biography of Ireland's Pirate Queen 1530–1603*. Dublin: Gill Books.

Chambers' Edinburgh Journal (1848). 'Savage Views of Civilisation' (24 June), p. 408. Available at: https://archive.org/details/chambersedinburg9to10cham/page/408/mode/2up.

Clark, Anna (1998). 'The Chevalier D'Eon and Wilkes: Masculinity and Politics in the Eighteenth Century', *Eighteenth-Century Studies* 32(1): 19–48.

Committee of Enquiry into the Education of Children from Ethnic Minority Backgrounds (1985). *The Swann Report*, p. 364. Available at: http://www.educationengland.org.uk/documents/swann/swann1985.html.

Connexion, The (2020). 'A Short History of Gemaine de Staël' (15 December). Available at: https://www.connexionfrance.com/Mag/Culture/A-short-history-of-Germaine-de-Stael-whose-ideas-laid-the-foundations-of-Romanticism-and-female-emancipation#:~:text='She%20teaches%20people%20to%20think,written%20by%20Madame%20de%20Sta%C3%ABl.

Corley, T. A. B. (1972). *Quaker Enterprise in Biscuits: Huntley and Palmers of Reading, 1822–1972*. London: Hutchinson.

Counsell, Christine (2004). 'Looking Through a Josephine Butler-shaped Window: Focusing Pupils' Thinking on Historical Significance', *Teaching History* 114: 30–34.

Counsell, Christine (2021). 'History'. In Alka Sehgal Cuthbert and Alex Standish (eds), *What Should Schools Teach?* 2nd edn. London: UCL Press, pp. 154–173.

Davies, Carole Boyce (2008). *Left of Karl Marx: The Political Life of Black Communist Claudia Jones*. Durham: Duke University Press.

Dawson, Ian (2003). *What is History? Year 7 Pupil's Book*. Glasgow: Hodder.

Defoe, Daniel (1726). *Mere Nature Delineated*. London: T. Warner.

Dennis, Nick (2016). 'Beyond Tokenism: Teaching a Diverse History in the Post-14 Curriculum', *Teaching History* 165: 37–41.

Dennis, Nick (2021). 'The Stories we Tell Ourselves: History Teaching, Powerful Knowledge and the Importance of Context'. In Arthur Chapman (ed.), *Knowing History in Schools: Powerful Knowledge and the Powers of Knowledge*. London: UCL Press, pp. 216–233.

Department for Education (2013). *History Programmes of Study: Key Stages 1 and 2*. Ref: DFE-00173-2013. Available at: https://assets.publishing.service.gov.uk/government/uploads/system/uploads/attachment_data/file/239035/PRIMARY_national_curriculum_-_History.pdf.

Department for Education (2013). *History Programmes of Study: Key Stage 3*. Ref: DFE-00194-2013. Available at: https://assets.publishing.service.gov.uk/government/uploads/system/uploads/attachment_data/file/239075/SECONDARY_national_curriculum_-_History.pdf.

De Staël, Germaine (1818). *Considerations on the Principal Events of the French Revolution*. New York: James Eastburn & Co. Available at: https://oll-resources.s3.us-east-2.amazonaws.com/oll3/store/titles/2212/Stael_1459.html.

De Staël, Germaine (1847). *Corinne, or Italy*, tr. Isabel Hill. London: Richard Bentley.

Dye, Eva Emery (1902). *The Conquest: The True Story of Lewis and Clark*. Chicago, IL: A. C. McClurg & Company.

Eberle, Roxanne (2002). *Chastity and Transgression in Women's Writing, 1792–1897*. Basingstoke: Palgrave.

Edwards, Judith (2017). *Fighting for Freedom: Abolitionists and Slave Resistance*. New York: Enslow Publishing.

Eisler, Benita (2013). *The Red Man's Bones: George Catlin, Artist and Showman*. New York: W.W. Norton & Company.

English Heritage (n.d.). 'Black Prisoners of War at Portchester Castle'. Available at: https://www.english-heritage.org.uk/visit/places/portchester-castle/history-and-stories/black-prisoners-at-portchester/.

English Heritage (n.d.). 'Sarah Forbes Bonetta, Queen Victoria's African Protégée'. Available at: https://www.english-heritage.org.uk/visit/places/osborne/history-and-stories/sarah-forbes-bonetta/.

English Heritage (n.d.). 'Walter Hungerford and the "Buggery Act"'. Available at: https://www.english-heritage.org.uk/learn/histories/lgbtq-history/walter-hungerford-and-the-buggery-act/.

English Heritage (2019). 'Speaking with Shadows: Transcript of Episode 2: The Caribbean Prisoners of Portchester Castle'. Available at: https://www.english-heritage.org.uk/siteassets/home/visit/inspire-me/speaking-with-shadows/sws-episode-2/speaking-with-shadows-episode-2-transcript.pdf.

Exeter Memories (2015). 'Gallows Cross – Heavitree' (27 July). Available at: http://www.exetermemories.co.uk/em/_places/gallows-cross.php.

Fontana, Biancamaria (2016). *Germaine de Staël: A Political Portrait.* Princeton, NJ: Princeton University Press.

Gent, Frank J. (1982). *The Trial of the Bideford Witches.* Bideford: Lazarus Press.

Glamorgan Monmouth and Brecon Gazette and Merthyr Guardian, The (1843). 'The Ojibbeway Indians at Windsor Castle' (30 December). Available at: https://newspapers.library.wales/view/3632965/3632967/.

Gove, Michael (2010). 'All pupils will learn our island story', Conservative Party conference [speech] (5 October). Available at: https://conservative-speeches.sayit.mysociety.org/speech/601441.

Green, Toby (2015). *History A: African Kingdoms: A Guide to the Kingdoms of Songhay, Kongo, Benin, Oyo and Dahomey c.1400–c.1800* [eBook]. Cambridge: OCR. Available at: https://www.ocr.org.uk/Images/208299-african-kingdoms-ebook-.pdf.

Hardage, Jeanette (2008). *Mary Slessor – Everybody's Mother: The Era and Impact of a Victorian Missionary.* Eugene, OR: Wipf and Stock.

Hartweg, Christine (2017). *Amy Robsart: A Life and its End.* Scotts Valley: CreateSpace Independent Publishing Platform.

Helmstadter, Richard J. and Lightman, Bernard (eds) (1990). *Victorian Faith in Crisis: Essays on Continuity and Chance in Nineteenth-Century Religious Belief.* Stanford: Stanford University Press.

Hoffenberg, Peter (2001). *An Empire on Display: English, Indian, and Australian Exhibitions from the Crystal Palace to the Great War.* Berkeley, CA: University of California Press.

Hogan, Anne and Bradstock, Andrew (eds) (1998). *Women of Faith in Victorian Culture: Reassessing the Angel in the House.* Basingstoke: Macmillan.

Humphries, Jane (2010). *Childhood and Child Labour in the British Industrial Revolution.* Cambridge: Cambridge University Press.

James, C. L. R. (2005). *Beyond a Boundary.* London: Yellow Jersey Press.

Jarboe, Andrew T. (2021). *Indian Soldiers in World War I: Race and Representation in an Imperial War.* Lincoln, NE: University of Nebraska Press.

Jones, Claudia (1949). 'An End to the Neglect of the Problems of the Negro Woman!' New York: National Women's Commission, p. 3. Available at: https://palmm.digital.flvc.org/islandora/object/ucf%3A4865.

Karkeek, Paul (2020 [1874]). *Devonshire Witches* [eBook]. Urbana, IL: Project Gutenberg. Available at: https://www.gutenberg.org/files/62273/62273.txt.

Kates, Gary (1995). 'The Transgendered World of the Chevalier/Chevalière d'Eon', *The Journal of Modern History* 67(3) (September): 558–594.

Kauffman, Miranda (2017). *Black Tudors: The Untold Story.* London: Oneworld Publications.

Keevil, J. J. (1957). 'Elizabeth Alkin "Alias" Parliament Joan', *Bulletin of the History of Medicine* 31(1): 17–28.

Kift, Dagmar (1996). *The Victorian Music Hall: Culture, Class and Conflict.* Cambridge: Cambridge University Press.

Kingsley, Charles (2008). *The Water-Babies: A Fairy Tale for a Land-Baby* [eBook]. Urbana, IL: Project Gutenberg. Available at: https://www.gutenberg.org/files/25564/25564-h/25564-h.htm.

Kister, Anna (n.d.). 'Biographical Notes: Jan Flisiak', *Hieronim Dekutowski.* Available at: https://www.hieronimdekutowski.pl/artykuly-znanych-autorow/noty-biograficzne-jan-flisiak-ps-chlopicki/.

Koonz, Claudia (1987). *Mothers in the Fatherland: Women, the Family and Nazi Politics.* London: Routledge.

Koven, Seth (2006). *Slumming: Sexual and Social Politics in Victorian London.* Princeton, NJ: Princeton University Press.

Lanceley, William (1925). *From Hall-Boy to House-Steward.* London: Edward Arnold & Co.

Levack, Brian P. (2013). *The Witch-Hunt in Early Modern Europe.* London: Routledge.

Lewis, Meriwether, Clark, William et al. (2005). 13 October 1805 entry. In Gary Moulton (ed.), *The Journals of the Lewis & Clark Expedition.* Lincoln, NE: University of Nebraska Press / University of Nebraska-Lincoln Libraries-Electronic Text Center. Available at https://lewisandclarkjournals.unl.edu/item/lc.jrn.1805-10-13.

Libes, Kenna (2020). '1778 – David Martin, Portrait of Dido Elizabeth Belle Lindsay and Lady Elizabeth Murray', *Fashion History Timeline* (3 August). Available at: https://fashionhistory.fitnyc.edu/1778-martin-dido-elizabeth/.

Lockyer, Bridget and Tazzymant, Abigail (2016). '"Victims of History": Challenging Students' Perceptions of Women in History', *Teaching History* 165: 8–15.

London, Jack (2009). *The People of the Abyss* [eBook]. Urbana, IL: Project Gutenberg. Available at: https://www.gutenberg.org/files/1688/1688-h/1688-h.htm.

Macintyre, Ben (2018). *The Spy and the Traitor.* London: Penguin.

Mandler, Peter (2015). 'History, National Life and the New Curriculum', *Schools History Project* (23 December). Available at: http://www.schoolshistoryproject.co.uk/ResourceBase/downloads/MandlerKeynote2013.pdf.

Marsh, Rob (2013). *Understanding Africa and the Events that Shaped its Destiny.* Johannesburg: LAPA.

Marwick, Arthur (1989). *The Nature of History.* New York: Macmillan.

Mathers, Helen (2014). *Patron Saint of Prostitutes: Josephine Butler and a Victorian Scandal.* Cheltenham: The History Press.

McLemee, Scott (ed.) (1996). *C. L. R. James on the 'Negro Question'.* Jackson, MS: University Press of Mississippi.

Mortimer, Ian (2017). *The Time Traveller's Guide to Restoration Britain.* London: Penguin.

Mukharji, T. N. (1886). *A Visit to Europe.* London: William Clowes & Sons.

National Archives, The (n.d.). 'Women and the English Civil Wars'. Available at: https://www.nationalarchives.gov.uk/education/resources/women-english-civil-wars/.

Nevitt, Marcus (2017). *Women and the Pamphlet Culture of Revolutionary England, 1640–1660.* London: Taylor & Francis.

O'Hara, Patricia (1997). '"The Woman of To-day": The Fin de Siècle Women of The Music Hall and Theatre Review', *Victorian Periodicals Review* 30(2): 141–156.

O'Leary, Naomi (2018). '"Her War Never Stopped": The Dutch Teenager who Resisted the Nazis', *The Guardian* (23 September). Available at: https://www.theguardian.com/world/2018/sep/23/freddie-oversteegen-dutch-teenager-who-resisted-nazis.

Olusoga, David (2014). *The World's War: Forgotten Soldiers of Empire.* Croydon: Head of Zeus.

Orr, Megan (2021). 'Ladylike in the Extreme: The Propagandism of Sarah Forbes Bonetta, Britain's 'African Princess' (2 December). Available at: https://scholarsarchive.byu.edu/cgi/viewcontent.cgi?article=1348&context=studentpub.

National, The (2016). 'A Parcel of Rogues: Jamie MacPherson: Making a Song and Dance over the Fate of Scotland's Robin Hood' (23 April). Available at: https://www.thenational.scot/news/14864804.a-parcel-of-rogues-jamie-MacPherson-making-a-song-and-dance-over-the-fate-of-scotlands-robin-hood/.

National Archives (n.d.). 'Women and the English Civil Wars'. Available at: https://www.nationalarchives.gov.uk/education/resources/women-english-civil-wars/.

Nicholson, Renton (1855). *The Lord Chief Baron Nicholson: An Autobiography.* London: George Vickers.

Parkes, Henry (1885). 'The Beauteous Terrorist', *The Libertarian Labyrinth.* Available at: https://www.libertarian-labyrinth.org/the-sex-question/sir-henry-parkes-the-beauteous-terrorist-sophie-perovskaya-1885/.

Parkinson, Justin (2016). 'The Significance of Sarah Baartman', *BBC News* (7 January). Available at: https://www.bbc.co.uk/news/magazine-35240987.

Parsons, Neil (1998). *King Khama, Emperor Joe and the Great White Queen*. Chicago, IL: University of Chicago Press.

Partington, Geoffrey (1980). *The Idea of an Historical Education*. Slough: NFER Publishing Company.

Pattinson, Juliette (2020). *Women of War: Gender, Modernity and the First Aid Nursing Yeomanry*. Manchester: Manchester University Press.

Pearson Education Limited (2021). *GCSE (9–1) History: Specification content: Paper 1 Option 13, Migrants in Britain, c800–Present and Notting Hill, c1948–c1970* (March). Available at: https://qualifications. pearson.com/content/dam/pdf/GCSE/History/2016/specification-and-sample-assessments/Pearson-Edexcel-GCSE-History-Migration-topic-final-draft.pdf.

Pop, Andrei (2011). 'Sympathetic Spectators: Henry Fuseli's Nightmare and Emma Hamilton's Attitudes', *Art History* 34(5) (November): 934–957.

Porter, David (1792). *Consideration on the Present State of Chimney Sweepers*. London: T. Burton.

Qureshi, Sadiah (2004). 'Displaying Sarah Baartman, the "Hottentot Venus"', *History of Science* 42(2): 233–257.

Roth, H. Ling (1903). *Great Benin: Its Customs, Art and Horrors*. Halifax: F. King.

Rothberg, Emma (2020). 'Lyda Conley', *National Women's History Museum*. Available at: https://www.womenshistory.org/education-resources/biographies/lyda-conley.

Royal Museums Greenwich (n.d.). 'Grace O'Malley: Pirate Queen of Ireland'. Available at: https://www.rmg.co.uk/stories/topics/grace-o-malley-irish-female-pirate.

Said, Edward (2016 [1978]). *Orientalism: Western Conceptions of the Orient*. London: Penguin.

Salars, Randy (2021). 'The Mystery of Buffalo Calf Road Woman', *Medium* (27 August). Available at: https://medium.com/illumination/the-mystery-of-buffalo-calf-road-woman-c6174f26288f.

Salkeld, Duncan (2012). *Shakespeare Among the Courtesans: Prostitution, Literature, and Drama, 1500–1650*. London: Routledge.

Shekhawat, Seema (2015). *Female Combatants in Conflict and Peace*. London: Palgrave Macmillan.

Simkin, John (1997). 'Sophia Perovskaya', *Spartacus Educational* (September). Available at: https://spartacus-educational.com/RUSperovskaya.htm.

Simkin, John (1997). 'Gertrud Scholtz-Klink', *Spartacus Educational* (September). Available at: https://spartacus-educational.com/GERscholtz.htm.

Singh, Kuldip (1996). 'Obituary: Aruna Asaf Ali', *The Independent* (30 July). Available at: https://www.independent.co.uk/news/people/obituary-aruna-asaf-ali-1331351.html.

Slide, Anthony (2012). *The Encyclopedia of Vaudeville*. Jackson, MS: University Press of Mississippi.

Sontag, Susan (1975). 'Fascinating Fascism', *New York Review of Books* (6 February). Available at: https://campus.albion.edu/gcocks/files/2013/08/Fascinating-Fascism.pdf.

Stead, W. T. (n.d.). 'Notice to our Readers: A Frank Warning', *W. B. Stead Resource Site*. First published in *The Pall Mall Gazette* (4 July 1885). Available at: https://www.attackingthedevil.co.uk/pmg/tribute/notice.php.

Stead, W. T. (n.d.). 'The Maiden Tribute of Modern Babylon I: The Report of our Secret Commission', *W. B. Stead Resource Site*. First published in *The Pall Mall Gazette* (6 July 1885). Available at: https://www.attackingthedevil.co.uk/pmg/tribute/mt1.php.

Swift, Jonathan (1726). *The Most Wonderful Wonder that Ever Appeared to the Wonder of the British Nation*. London: G. Faulkner.

Taylor, Becky (2014). *Another Darkness, Another Dawn: A History of Gypsies, Roma and Travellers*. London: Reaktion.

Thompson, E. P. (1991). *The Making of the English Working Class*. London: Penguin.

Thompson Tetreault, Mary Kay (1986). 'Integrating Women's History: The Case of United States History High School Textbooks', *The History Teacher* 19(2): 211–262.

Turner, David (2012). *Disability in Eighteenth-Century England*. Abingdon: Routledge.

University of Southampton Special Collections (2017). 'Richard Cockle Lucas 1800–1883: Talented Artist and Engaging Eccentric' (6 September). Available at: https://specialcollectionsuniversityofsouthampton.wordpress.com/2017/09/06/richard-cockle-lucas-1800-1883-talented-artist-and-engaging-eccentric/.

Wardle, Thomas (1886). *Colonial and Indian Exhibition, 1886.* London: William Clowes & Sons.

Waterman, Hillary (2015). 'Licoricia of Winchester, Jewish Widow and Medieval Financier', *JSTOR Daily* (28 October). Available at: https://daily.jstor.org/licoricia-jewish-medieval-women-moneylenders/.

Watson, Bruce (2002). 'George Catlin's Obsession', *Smithsonian Magazine* (December). Available at: https://www.smithsonianmag.com/arts-culture/george-catlins-obsession-72840046/.

Williams, Kate (2007). *England's Mistress: The Infamous Life of Emma Hamilton.* London: Arrow.

Williams, Wendy (2020). *Windrush Lessons Learned Review* (March), p. 7. Ref: ISBN 978-1-5286-1779-6. Available at: https://assets.publishing.service.gov.uk/government/uploads/system/uploads/attachment_data/file/876336/6.5577_HO_Windrush_Lessons_Learned_Review_LoResFinal.pdf.

Worsley, Lucy (2011). 'Peter the Wild Boy', *The Public Domain Review* (7 November). Available at: https://publicdomainreview.org/essay/peter-the-wild-boy.

Yenen, Alp (2014). 'Legacies of Jihad 100 Years after World War I', *Gingko Library* (14 November). Available at: https://edoc.unibas.ch/40784/1/20180323110905_5ab4d24164d65.pdf.